The Gig Economy in India

The Gig Economy in India explores the topic of gig work in India's digital political economy, and the relationship between key factors such as start-ups, state governments, and platform providers.

The book begins by placing the gig economy in context, defining the platform ecosystem and the Indian government's perception of its problems and opportunities. Thomas then examines the critical dimensions of the gig economy in India, from its data infrastructure capabilities, the enabling role of venture capitals and FinTech, to government regulations. Attention is paid to the precarity of gig labour, the vagaries of algorithmic management, and the minimal legal support available for workers. The book also includes chapters on labour resistance and highlights some of the issues related to the ethics of artificial intelligence.

Given the limited research on India as a case study, this volume fills a crucial gap in the literature. It will interest scholars in diverse fields such as business management, digital media, and communication studies.

Pradip Ninan Thomas is at the School of Arts and Communications at the University of Queensland, Australia. He is the author of 12 books, including *Information Infrastructures in India: The Long View (2022)* and *Platform Regulation: Exemplars, Approaches and Solutions (2023).*

The Gig Economy in India
Start-Ups, Infrastructure and Resistance

Pradip Ninan Thomas

Routledge
Taylor & Francis Group
LONDON AND NEW YORK

First published 2025
by Routledge
4 Park Square, Milton Park, Abingdon, Oxon OX14 4RN

and by Routledge
605 Third Avenue, New York, NY 10158

Routledge is an imprint of the Taylor & Francis Group, an informa business

British Library Cataloguing-in-Publication Data
A catalogue record for this book is available from the British Library

ISBN: 978-1-032-79374-0 (hbk)
ISBN: 978-1-032-79375-7 (pbk)
ISBN: 978-1-003-49170-5 (ebk)

DOI: 10.4324/9781003491705

Typeset in Galliard
by SPi Technologies India Pvt Ltd (Straive)

Contents

Introduction
The Platform Economy in India

This volume attempts to assess the gig economy (GE) and its political economy in relation to gig workers, their management and resistance within what can broadly be termed an algorithmically driven mode of production. It deals with these issues in the context of India's embrace of a digital present and future and the technocratic visions, ambitions and achievements of the Government of India (GoI) to become a knowledge economy through its multiple, mission-level connectivity projects. India Stack is now being marketed to governments interested in the potential for the scalability, replicability, adaptability and adoptability of the hardware and software architectures linked to Digital India. The sheer magnitude of these projects in a population-rich, topographically diverse country such as India is quite astounding. India has the benefit of an army of relatively young, technological professionals who have the knowledge and skills to design and execute national mission–level connectivity projects. Unfortunately, though, the nature of their education is such that few have the curiosity or commitment to an understanding of the social consequences of such projects that go beyond the government-speak of national access, connectivity and financial inclusion. The GE is of course an aspect of the larger platform economy in India the embrace of which is multi-sectoral and ambit extensive and involves the transactional habits of citizens on state and private platforms.

The Platform Ecosystem

It is important that we understand the different components of the platform ecosystem. In a study of Reliance Jio, a company that belongs to the much larger mega-corporation Reliance Industries, Athique and Kumar (2022:1431) make a distinction between two levels of the platform ecosystem:

"Technical ecosystem: The range of interlocking technologies, resources, infrastructures and processes that ensure interoperable platform architecture – including raw materials, energy, buildings, processors, data storage, satellites, sensors, cables, spectrum, algorithms, interface device and operating systems.

DOI: 10.4324/9781003491705-1

Business ecosystem: The interlocking relationships and interdependencies that determine the business environment of digital platform: including capital and investment interests, company structures, subsidiaries, suppliers, business partners, product ranges, cross-subsidization and tie-ups, market information, workforce, plant, data assets, intellectual property, and market regulators".

In the case of India, these two ecosystems are critically dependent on the political ecosystem and the State/GoI that has played a major role in investing, planning, establishing and regulating these ecosystems. In fact, the writ of the central government and local state governments is key to the understanding of the platform ecosystem in India as policy framers, investors, planners, suppliers, establishing public–private partnerships, suppliers of infrastructure such as data centre parks and essential infrastructure such as electricity and water supply, making available land, legal frameworks, business-friendly policies for start-ups and other tech ventures, tax exemptions, seed funding, loans, incubators along with political will that is critical to such ventures (See StartupIndia). It is useful to also distinguish between the large public and private sector platforms that provide infrastructural services that are foundational and the sectoral platforms that build their services on the back of these infrastructural platforms (See van Dijk, et al.: 2018, 4). India Stack taken in its entirety can be seen as a foundational infrastructure that facilitates and enables many sectoral platforms including fintech and other platforms. India Stack consists of digital public platforms that are based on open standards, open application programming interfaces (APIs) and data interoperability. Jacquline Hicks (2020:331) in an article on India Stack poses three questions on the political economy of platforms, answers to which are critical to understanding the larger objectives of India Stack:

- How do businesses profit from India Stack? What commercial imperatives are driving it forward?
- How significant is India Stack as a profit-making system? Is it likely to endure?
- What sort of business–state relationships surround it? What are its implications for the relations between state, business and labour?

It would be reasonable to assume that the future of the digital and increasingly artificial intelligence (AI)-driven mode of development in India is secure and that its deployments will lead to economic efficiencies, growth and production across a variety of sectors. However, AI needs to be seen as an important, emerging technology in the context of Indian reality characterised by older and newer modes of production including agriculture, manufacturing along with the many informal modes of production. The challenge for the Indian government is to invest in all these modes of production precisely because large numbers of people survive through working in the economies that are ancillary, tangentially linked or critically related to these modes of production. In the recent decade or two, however, there has been a shift in the public commitments made by the GoI to these sectors and a perception that their only real interest is investments in a mode of production associated with digital platforms. Economic growth associated with other modes of production such as manufacturing and agriculture is stagnant or suboptimal. There is a quiet and largely invisible agrarian crisis unfolding in India resulting in a migration to cities by young people who inevitably become a part of migrant labour involved in a variety of gig work in the informal economy. While there is a case to be made for national connectivity, questions related to the why and what of connectivity remain largely unanswered. What happens after connectivities are achieved? Are there enabling environments in place that will help translate connectivity to health and education into qualitative differences in the lives of people? Or is connectivity an end that is primarily related to the expansion of governmentality? Is the increase in gig work linked to platforms a cause for celebration or does it merely push us to think the reality of shrinking places for work in the formal economy at the expense of work in a burgeoning informal economy?

The Role of the State

A key player in this unfolding narrative is the State, or as it is referred to in this volume, the GoI that itself has become platformised and is invested in transforming India into an AI economy, a cashless country where every Indian is an aspirational digital native armed with a credit card and a bank account. This vision of digital solutionism is imprinted onto every national mission–level connectivity project of which there are many. Vijayanka Nair (2019:523) describes this new state in the making as a 'start-up state'.

> Neither fully state, nor fully start-up, the start-up state is (in) a state of becoming. In using the term "start-up state", I am pointing to three things. One, that as a platform for start-ups, the start-up state integrates an *ab initio* and largely technological approach to socioeconomic problems. This would-be state is unencumbered by the pedantry and proceduralism of the post-colonial state. Two, that every time a start-up melds with the state, the fusing configures the state as an entity born anew. Even as Aadhaar architects were careful to maintain that a start-up must reintegrate into government, officials keenly communicated to me that Aadhaar, revolutionary as it was, could "completely transform" the state. It is plausible to suggest, then, that the start-up state is a state permanently *in potentia*. As it encounters challenges, the state forges start-ups, which in turn regenerate the state; the process continues ad infinitum.

The Indian State's transformation from its involvement in the redistribution of survival resources to a platform intermediary linking customers to services is an ongoing process that is reflected in the initiatives linked to India Stack (See Rao: 2019).

A Brief Introduction to the Relationship between the State and Big Tech in India

Let me at the outset describe what this book is about and why. For readers who are not familiar with India, in spite of all the economic reforms beginning in the early 1990s and the steady march of privatisation, the State/GoI continues to play a paramount role in shaping the contours of the Indian economy. I am not suggesting that the influence of Big Tech – such as Google, Meta and Amazon is inconsequential. They play an extraordinarily important role although their power is constrained and is to some extent subservient to the power of the Indian state that benefits from their relationship with Big Tech but that is also in a position to dictate what Big Tech can and cannot do. At any given time, the State is involved in a number of litigations against Big Tech, regulating Big Tech and also involved in creating infrastructures to enable competition and a level playing field. The State is dependent on them as is the case with Cloud and Data Centres (See Chapter 4) although it is also involved in contesting and curbing their hegemonic aspirations (Singh:2021). In other words, the State's relationship with Big Tech is in some ways like the relationship between the European Union (EU) and Big Tech although this relationship is arguably more ambivalent (See Thomas:2023). Urvashi Aneja and Angelina Chamuah (2020:6) have argued that Big Tech is best described as a concept rather than a static group of companies. The concept is based on four shared features. These are firms that are based on a data-centric model of growth, succeed through the achievement of network effects, play an infrastructural role and are involved in a variety of consumer-oriented civic functions including news, products and socialities. In the Indian context, apart from 1) major global Big Tech firms such as Google and Microsoft, there are also 2) local Big Tech firms such as Reliance Jio and Flipkart, 3) a host of Indian fintech and other firms across every productive sector routinely referred to as start-ups including firms such as Uber and Swiggy that are part of the GE and 4) the Indian state that is involved in the establishment of nation-wide digital infrastructure projects that are now being marketed to the rest of the world. In other words, the platform economy in India consists of actors involved at these four levels. The GoI has a complex relationship with these actors that has been shaped in the recent past by its nationalistic, Made in India rhetoric, its aspirational logic of becoming a 'cashless society', a knowledge superpower and a leader in AI-based innovation. At the same time, aspirational India has to reckon with the fact that in order to play the tech game, India simply has to also become a semiconductor, chip-superpower that it currently is not.

There has arguably been a shift in the exercise of power from the analogue era when the Indian State had a monopoly over its power over citizens to a context in which this power is shared by the State and the players involved in the platform economy in India. There is a sense in which machine learning and AI along with the control over infrastructure and logistics (See Rossiter:2016) offer both the State and platforms power over citizens and consumers. I have written about this power over workers exerted by platforms in Chapter 5 (AI, Machine Learning and Gig Workers in India) and over the control of logistics in Chapter 7 (Cloud, Data Centres and the Politics of Infrastructure). Keller Easterling (2014:15) writes about the history of this power that began with Special Economic Zones and IT Corridors where tech firms were guaranteed access to non-unionised labour and were exempted from labour and environmental laws. In Keller's words

> As a site of multiple, overlapping, or nested forms of sovereignty, where domestic and transnational jurisdictions collide, infrastructure *space* becomes a medium of what might be called *extrastatecraft* – a portmanteau describing the often undisclosed activities outside of, in addition to, and sometimes in partnership with statecraft.

Arguably, a host of tech firms in India with the State and on their own are involved in the exercise of this extrastatecraft often with the tacit support of technocrats who act as brokers for multiple projects linked with aspirational India.

Regulatory Arbitrage

One of the issues that rather directly deals with this question of workers' rights is the reality of 'regulatory arbitrage', the role played by platforms in carving out the rules of gig work in the absence of any prior regulatory knowledge and a regulatory vacuum that is only now being investigated. The power of Big Tech, a handful of tech giants, to monetise and control transactional data is immense and their consolidated power over the global economy has been unprecedented. This has given them the power to determine the rules of work and in that process minimise their responsibility to their workers, who as 'partners' and as 'self-employed' gig workers do not qualify for compensation and rights under labour laws that only apply to full-time workers in the organised sectors. In other words, these platforms have created their own nomenclature to describe their role as third parties mediating the delivery of services to customers. They have gone to great lengths to describe their role as mere brokers although this has been called out in some jurisdictions such as the EU where they have been forced to reckon with their role in managing employer–employee relationships.

There are those who would argue that the technological glitches in the operations of the GE are to be expected given the relative newness of this enterprise. While not discounting such views, the GoI's techno-optimism is founded on an infrastructural imaginary and the all-sufficiency of techno-solutions for the many 'wicked' problems facing its citizenry. In other words, the GoI believes that banking on technology is an end in itself. At the very same time, the GoI seems to have taken the position that in a data-driven context, there simply has to be trade-offs between privacy and individual rights against the imperative of national connectivity projects (See Mishra:2019). However, these trade-offs also include ignoring the need for an ethical framework for the use of AI and/or the need to assess its 'risk' in the interest of nurturing India's competitive edge in this area. The consequences of such trade-offs are particularly reflected in the security of data given the many mission-level connectivity projects that involve the generation and collection of personal data. India has experienced multiple data breaches in a context in which there are also other tech-based deficits including the routinisation of the algorithmic mismanagement of workers in the GE and the consistent downplaying of the need for data privacy. In other words, I argue in this volume that such trade-offs are detrimental and inimical to the larger interests of the Indian population whose data is now stored in cloud and data centres owned primarily by Big Tech (Chapter 4). The fundamental issue in India is of course that of a country characterised by multiple fissures across race and class, caste and gender and rich and poor. These fissures are also faultlines – and the question then is one of how to implement digital democracy in a country in which such divides limit the quality of digital inclusion. In other words, connectivity per se is no guarantee of digital democracy and is an objective of the many mission-level connectivity projects in education, health, financial inclusion and others.

The Infrastructural Moment

This volume also deals with some of the infrastructures that are critical to lives lived in transactional environments – data and cloud centres that have become increasingly indispensable to data storage which is a vital sector in any consideration of the platform complex. Data generated by Uber, Swiggy and other platforms often find their way to these large data storage facilities along with data generated by the many mission-level, public sector projects. It is intriguing that there is a massive gap between the rhetoric of self-sustainability, self-reliance (*Atmanirbhar*), data localisation and Made in India and the reality of hyper-cloud centres being owned by companies such as Amazon Web Services (AWS) and Microsoft Azure that have become the preferred storage destination for the large chunks of transactional data generated by both privately owned platforms and the Central and state governments through their e-government and other connectivity projects. This seems to be an error of judgement although it could also be an admission that India simply does not have indigenously-owned capacities to store such large amounts of data. There is an infrastructural deficit in India and Big Tech is playing an important role in the storage and management of public data. It highlights the reality of public–private partnerships in India that are flourishing in spite of the public rhetoric related to regulating Big Tech. Big Tech solutionism is a practical reality in India. This volume also explores the role played by the private sector in fulfilling India's vision with respect to this deficit and its contribution to Digital India. I did, in a previous volume

Information Infrastructures in India (2022), explore key communication/information infrastructures in India although not data centres. In some ways, I am glad that I did not include work on cloud and data infrastructures in that book as it fits in well with an understanding of the larger ecology related to the GE in India. There is an excellent edited volume *Data Infrastructures in India* (2022:2) edited by Manish K Jha and Ritam Sengupta that offers a critical introduction to data centres described as 'infrastructural entities that are both "things" and "relations between things"' that are critical to state and private enterprises involved in logistical coordination.

Gig Workers

This volume explores the GE in India and workers in the GE who increasingly are being embraced by AI in their lives and livelihoods. Much of the work that they do is contingent and based on independent contracting. Key to this work is the platform as an intermediary that enables the supply and demand of labour and that is involved in shaping and controlling an algorithmically managed labour market. AI has had a disruptive impact on the lives of workers in a context in which delivery and ride-hail platforms have evolved their own, limited attempts at self-regulation that quite fundamentally do not provide a framework that is supportive of the interests and rights of workers. In other words, one of the areas that I have tried to address in this volume is the consequences of platformised work for gig workers' lives and livelihoods that have not been thought through and their evolving resistance to what are opaque and non-transparent working conditions. If, as it is projected, more and more people in India join this labour force, its consequences need to be fully explored for workers in terms of wages, work conditions and security and the responsibilities to these workers by the GoI and platform organisations clarified. The issue related to consequences can also be applied to an understanding of the larger unorganised sector, of which gig workers are but a small part. This volume also explores issues related to gig workers and their work that are increasingly being circumscribed by algorithmic fiat and the incipient resistance by some of these gig workers to their working conditions and terms of employment. Gig workers are by no means new to India given that they really belong to the unorganised sector. This sector accounts for 85 per cent or more of employment in India – in agriculture, manufacturing, small firms and increasingly as migrant labour who service cities in their capacities as domestic workers, security personnel, vendors, etc. And yet, platform-linked gig workers are in some ways different because their work as flexible workers is computationally controlled and transactionally managed by bots. The growing resistance of gig workers in the platform economy to the vagaries of their management and the gamification of their livelihoods is an important moment in the history of the working classes involved in gig work.

Digital Solutionism

On the one hand, the transformative potential of the digital simply has to be harnessed and operationalised at the national and local levels. This is a categorical imperative. The contributions made by this sector are critical to growth and productivity in India and arguably some of the wealth that is created in this sector contributes to India's extensive welfare economy. Digital efficiencies do contribute to the creation of economic value and the many disintermediations that are a consequence of the adoption of digital means do occasionally contribute to agency and empowerment. However, we need to also acknowledge that the task of creating a cashless society that may or may not succeed is on a completely different level from the imperative of creating a casteless society and a society where justice and rights are for all as per constitutional guarantees. It would seem that the realisation of this latter project is immensely complicated despite guarantees and evidence of multiple rights enshrined in a cornucopia of legislative measures. The GoI and their technocratic base believe that access to digital devices such as a smartphones by every Indian will act as the great leveller that will magically result in the disappearance of hierarchies and the dissolution of exclusivities based on caste, class, gender and other divides. This digital solutionism was on display during the COVID pandemic where smart technologies were deployed to contain the spread of the illness. "Contact tracing and quarantining apps were pushed into mobile phones supported by CCTV and drone surveillance, google map tracking, as well as AI, facial recognition and predictive analytics. Cities were zoned into red, orange and green areas based on infection rates and Integrated Command and Control Centers (ICCC) in 45 of the 100 smart cities were repurposed into "COVID-19 War Rooms" (Dutta, et al. 2020:382). Academics call this complete embrace of technology 'technological determinism', a pathological condition that is reflected in a belief in technologies disrupting and shaping tradition and old ways of doing things and, in this case, replacing it with the largesse and transformative logic associated with the digital sublime. In the case of COVID, in particular, the platforms used were not robust and, as has been highlighted elsewhere in this chapter, led to multiple data leaks. I am not suggesting that technologies do not have the capacity to change societies. They do, and have, such as the successive technological revolutions of steam and electricity that have occurred over the last three centuries and that have contributed to the shaping of lives, livelihoods, new modes of production and labour and social change. However, these revolutions were accompanied by major struggles between capital and labour that resulted in many articulations of workers' rights that are today enshrined in labour laws. In the era of the digital mode of production and the platform economy, the decline in trade unionism, the growth of the unorganised sector and the globalisation of neoliberal forms of growth, the rights of workers have become a secondary concern to the imperative of growth at all costs. In fact, one of the distinctive features of the GE is the reality of minimal or no labour ties. As Galan & Zuniga-Vicente (2022:6–7) observe in a chapter on the GE

> The GE does not create labor ties between the different parties. The relationships exclusively linked to a specific project/task/activity. Once the project/task/activity ends, the relationship ends. There are no obligations on either the progenitor of the project/task/activity or the person providing the service. Both parties have to agree upon the value of this.

So one of the questions that has been raised in this volume but perhaps only provisionally dealt with is why this is the case in labour-rich India. Workers in the GE who are celebrated in NITI Aayog's report on the GE have been consistently denied basic human rights such as the rights to a living wage, good working conditions, social security and even the freedom of association. In 2017, following Ola/Uber driver strikes across major cities in India for better fares, the Delhi High Court in a ruling denied these workers the freedom to associate because the workers were seen as independent contractors and not as employees. The court issued a 'permanent injunction' to workers linked to two taxi driver unions, the Sarvodaya Driver's Association of Delhi and the Rajdhani Tourist Driver's Union (Mishra:2017).

There is a population that is being cajoled into connectivity but who remains in the background as welfare recipients in the unorganised sector and as gig workers. These populations are not the beneficiaries of the new India in the making but are the labourers involved in creating India's heaven on earth. They played a key role as frontline workers during the COVID pandemic in India, taking immense risks delivering food during lockdowns resulting in a profit upturn for food delivery and other platforms. Many died from COVID (Raj & Gurmat: 2021). It is of course well known that India is a country that is characterised by many disparities – economic and social. Gig workers belong to the 'unorganised' sector that accounts for the bulk of employment in India. Will they ever benefit from being workers paid a consistent salary, full social security and rights as they contribute to the vision of Digital India or will they remain at the mercy of platforms, the vagaries of algorithmic management and a GoI that is yet to show any urgency in how to respond to the needs of these workers? Will the GoI fulfil its duties to all workers in India, including those working in the service of the platform economy? While gig workers are connected, this is arguably only in a tangential sense, connectivity is a precondition and essential to their work as platform workers. It is extraordinary that these marginal workers are now serviced by fintech platforms who are often in tie-ups with food delivery and ride-hail platforms to offer these workers loans very much like money lenders did in a previous era.

We do of course need to acknowledge that there are a minority of digital nomads involved in remote work whose educational background and skills position them perfectly to execute high-paying, piecemeal work in India and abroad. The majority though in the gig labour economy are involved in work as flexible labour in a context in which this flexibility is controlled by algorithms and managed remotely. While the flexibility of gig work is often celebrated, this needs to be seen not just in terms of Uber drivers driving when they are so inclined but also in the reality of controlled flexibility in which the options for workers are circumscribed by AI. If they drive less and are immune to the nudgings to earn more on their gamified dashboard, the earnings made for every trip could well decline. This then is one of the conundrums related to the platform society. On the one hand, technological change offers new opportunities for self-realisation and network effects and increased user participation can contribute to economic growth. However, I think that, on the other hand, it is hugely optimistic to believe that there are correspondences between network externalities and bridgings of social and other divides, such as caste; the latter has existed over millennia and it is difficult to dislodge through technological interventions. More likely than not, new technologies tend to become domesticated by the dominant social, and this is highlighted in the operationalisations of algorithmic management in the economic management of gig workers (For a well-written introduction to, and a critique of the Digital Platform Economy in India, see Sasikumar & Sersia: 2020).

Risk, Regulation and Data Leaks

Much of what is happening in India in the context of the GE including start-ups, investments made by venture capitalists in fintech and other platform-based services is being done in the context of relatively little or no regulatory oversight. Despite the DPDPA (2023), there is a lack of clarity on data protection and privacy to speak of in India and this gap has provided the perfect opportunity for data aggregators to flourish since the legal basis for the protection of transactional data generated by individuals is rudimentary, at best. So, the ownership of data remains an issue. In its absence, the State has become the de facto owner of personal data transacted over its platforms – data that is gathered without consent and that is being traded and sold to third parties. India is a data haven, a Wild West characterised by an absence of data ethics. While the GoI has asserted that it will not work towards a separate law on AI, unlike the European Commission which has clear guidelines on AI based on risk levels, this 'welcome to sandbox India for all your AI needs' approach is potentially harmful given the realities of both responsible and irresponsible AI and the difficulties in policing AI applications in India. The GoI tends to be defensive about data breaches such as the CoWin data breach in June 2023 which is the third data breach linked to the same site since 2021 (Covid Database:2023). Between 2018 and 2023, there have been 47 data leaks and 142 incidents of data breaches in India (The Wire:2023). There are real, material consequences from data leaks and breaches. Jean Dreze and Reetika Khera (2022) highlight six issues related to Aadhar that have resulted in exclusions of already vulnerable populations – excessive Aadhar imposition, arbitrary exclusions, inadequate facilities for Aadhar enrolment, updation and retrieval, unreliable demographic details, error-ridden Aadhar payment bridge system and most worryingly fraud-prone Aadhar-enabled payment system. "The Aadhaar-enabled Payment System, or

AePS, is a facility that enables someone who has an Aadhaar-linked account to withdraw money from it anywhere in India through biometric authentication with a 'business correspondent' – a kind of mini-ATM. There have been rampant abuses of this facility by corrupt business correspondents, especially "roaming business correspondents", to extort money from unsuspecting victims by persuading them to put their finger in a point-of-sale machine under some pretext. The prime targets of corrupt business correspondents are defenceless people such as elderly persons without education". Such writings indicate that the GoI, while keen on the economic contributions from AI to the Gross development product (GDP), is not invested to the extent that it ought to be in matters such as data privacy and data security. The issue of Aadhar security/insecurity is highlighted most comprehensively in the work and findings of computer programmer and cybersecurity researcher Anand Venkatanaraynan. In a number of public presentations, he has described the other side of India Stack – what he calls Fraud Stack and the ways in which this parallel ecosystem works in India. He has described the processes of fraud, its political economy and has especially explored the ways in which it has been used all over India to enrol people on the Aadhar database. Venkatanarayan (See Excel sheet list of Aadhar Fraud:2017) has traced the increase in Aadhar fraud to the decision to shutting down 50,000 enrolment operators for violating Aadhar processing guidelines (50,000 Aadhar enrolment: TOI), some of whom were subsequently involved in 'enrolment for bribes' scams (Venkatanarayan:2018). What is alarming about these exposes is the fact that every process – from biometric ID to KYC (know your customer) has been corrupted. As he has pointed out after investigating a number of Aadhar scams

> the UP Aadhaar hack case, provided the first glimpse into how the fraudsters managed to disable the security features and also defeat the back end data analytics. The offline nature of data acquisition provided a window large enough to compromise the data quality of the biometric templates and the identity documents without getting detected for at least a year. Further the streamlining of the process of data acquisition, made it very hard to stop the deployment and further usage of the compromised software even today, thus illustrating the problem of data acquisition at scale with good quality.
>
> (See Venkatanarayanan: 2019)

Silvia Masiero and Viktor Arvidson (2019) in an article on the unintended consequences of technology highlight what they term 'degenerative' outcomes stemming from Aadhar's incorporation into the Public Distribution System (PDS). They point to evidence of ***exclusion*** from access because of issues with authentication, ***distortion*** from selective monitoring that is focussed on ration dealers but not on the transportation or storage phases, and ***redirection***, the planned shift from PDS to cash transfers (916). We do not have country-level data on the volume of exclusions, on the nature and levels of leakage owing to fraud in the food distribution chain nor information on how the shift to cash transfers will impact people's ability to buy food and grain within a context characterised by an agricultural free market. India is in the throes of 'Aadhar creep', the steady IDisation of everything including most recently, in the registration of births and deaths (Livemint:2023). Arguably, Digital India and its dark underside consisting of data leakage, scammers and phishing, digital extortions, surveillance, trade-in private data and a top-heavy approach to privacy are constitutive. In other words, as all Indian citizens are being funnelled into enacting data-centric enactments of consumption and citizenship, there are parallel processes dedicated to exploiting data vulnerabilities resulting in various gradations of data subversions. Investments in furthering the 'aspirational' ambitions of Digital India need to be accompanied by investments in mitigating the various digital 'insecurities' that ordinary people in India are now faced with.

I have found India's engagement with the digital a fascinating journey. I have written extensively on this journey beginning with India's early success with software followed by business process outsourcing and the turn towards the platform economy (See Thomas: 2012, 2019, 2023). It has been a story of vision and ambition, the harnessing of digital solutions in the creation of land records, business process outsourcing and content moderation, connectivity and access, fintech and the cashless society, investments in closing the digital divide, surveillance, multiple national mission-level projects, smartphones, Digital India and India Stack, platforms and AI, COVID acceleration of platform-based consumption along with deficits that include a reputation for the most internet shutdowns, data breaches and a lackadaisical approach to data privacy. A number of national mission–level projects have been successfully operationalised, although the larger objectives of some of these projects, such as Aadhar, remain shrouded in opacity. The question of who benefits from all these investments remains an important one. As India transforms itself into a knowledge economy and creates nation-wide, mission-level connectivity projects that question requires a credible answer. While India is home to an economically powerful middle class, many of whom are resource rich and have the means to avail themselves of all the benefits that connectivity brings, for most Indians, whether or not they have a data plan, welfare connectivities are critical to their everyday survival. The gig workers in this volume are also those for whom connectivity is critical to their work. They are involved in servicing the GE and labouring for platforms who are involved in using algorithmic management to increase their 'accumulation by dispossession', a term used by critical geographer David Harvey (2005) to describe the nature of predatory capitalism.

So this volume fundamentally is a critical introduction to this new economy in the making. It focuses specifically on gig workers working for food delivery and ride-hail platforms, their captivity to algorithmic management and their resistance. There are other platforms such as those that are involved in brokering homework and whose productivity is linked to different versions of algorithmically-managed labour that I do not deal with in this volume. While this volume does not account for the variety of platforms and labour relationships, it nevertheless offers a view of a specific sector of the GE in India, its relationship to the State, the private sector and its contribution to the development of data capitalism in India. While the volume does highlight the different forms of resistance that exist in India, my belief is that gig worker unions can use the strength of their membership to create counter-vailing power and to demand a range of securities for gig workers from both the GoI and platforms. Jamie Woodcock and Mark Graham in their 2020 volume *The Gig Economy: A Critical Introduction* highlight four essential principles that are key to the rights of workers in the GE – transparency, accountability, worker power and democratic ownership (118–140). There are indications that there are positive developments in these four areas in India although issues related to the unorganised sector in India are both extensive and complex. What the volume does is highlight the visions and ambitions of the GoI with respect to platforms and start-ups along with the challenges that it faces with the implementation of its policies and principles in practice.

As an unrepentant political economist of communications, I have over the years and in my writings consistently explored the gaps between the principle and the practice of information and communication. Critical writings on India's embrace of AI are necessary precisely because academics tend to ignore or only superficially deal with deep and complex political-economy-related issues linked to India's embrace of the platform economy, gig work and AI futures. There is a marked tendency to celebrate connectivity for its own sake and to deal with the successes of technique over the need to contextualise technique within the boundaries of political economy. The story of India Stack is quite critically about India's prowess and ambitions as a technology leader. This story is also entwined in the present government's nationalist rhetoric that clearly positions India as a superpower on par with its rivals China and USA. This vision arguably is in place for the consumption of its middle classes who are after all the key demographic that provides the legitimacy that the GoI is interested in. So it is not surprising that during PM Modi's visit to the USA in June 2023 that he met Elon Musk who has promised that Teslas would be sold in India and Sundar Pichai of Google who has promised investing in a global fintech centre in the PM's home state Gujarat. Arguably though, this vision falls short when it comes to the welfare of digital workers who for all practical purposes face the very same issues faced by other workers in the unorganised sector.

The furore over ChatGPT became an intensely mediated issue during the time that I was involved in writing this volume. The Italian government even went as far as banning ChatGPT although most governments viewed this innovation as a challenge and opportunity that needed to be dealt with within regulated environments. In the university environment that I belong to in Brisbane, Australia, the immediate issue was with the impact of generative AI on student work and in particular with potential ethical issues linked to content generated by ChatGPT submitted/passed off as original work attributable to the student. This certainly remains of concern although I am personally bemused by the response of universities given that ChatGPT is just a teaser for more complex problems that will arise because of AI and that will have implications for the future of the university and education in general. I end this introduction with the issue of ChatGPT because it is the latest example of a disruptive AI-based innovation that has consequences that we are yet to figure out. The question really is one of whether we the GoI will ignore such challenges or have the collective will to enable AI to flourish within a set of ethical parameters established through a multi-stakeholder process.

The following chapter synopsis provides a succinct introduction to the chapters in this volume.

1 **Introduction**: The opening chapter places the GE and gig work in context. It attempts to define the platform ecosystem, the paramount role played by the State, the nature of regulatory arbitrage and the consequences of the trade-offs between a platformising state and its less-than-satisfactory approach to data security and data management. It highlights India's techno-optimism expressed most spectacularly in India Stack and the GoI's vision of connectivity as an end in itself. It also deals with the limits of this vision and the fact that in a complexly diverse country, there are significant limits to techno-solutionism. It concludes by assessing the prospects for gig workers in this vision of techno-plenty.
2 **India Stack, Techno-Optimism and Platform Contradictions**: This chapter, following on from the introduction explores the vision, nature and implementation of India Stack which is the edifice and foundation on which fintech and other platforms are being built. It deals with the Holy Grail of financial inclusion and the consequences of data breaches that throw light on the privacy-lite approach adopted by the GoI. The NITI Aayog Report on India's booming GE is highlighted and critically evaluated as an example of the techno-optimism that abounds in India. It deals with the optimistic take in the report on gig workers, their prospects and projections related to the security of gig workers that is yet to become a reality. The chapter concludes with a look at some of the key features of India's digital economy.
3 **The Governance/Mis-Governance of Start-Ups**: This chapter explores the start-up economy in India. Beginning with an analysis of two corporate scandals, the unravelling of the ed-tech firm Byju's and the Hindenburg Report related to the Adani, the chapter deals with the challenges related to governance faced by this sector and corporate India. It highlights the ambitions of India to become a 'start-up' state, the challenges faced by the Competitions Commission of India and the implications of the Digital Personal Data Protection Act (DPDPA) for start-ups. It makes a case for a larger reckoning with the start-up economy that also includes cyber-scammers and cyber-criminals. The chapter concludes by highlighting the start-up state's responsibilities in the context of persistent realities such as poverty.

4 **Venture Capitalism, Informality and the Gig Economy**: This chapter explores the nature of venture capitalism in relation to the GE in India, the enabling environment that supports such capital and the specific example of fintech as an illustration of the workings of this sector. This story of start-ups is contrasted with an analysis of the informal economy and the nature of the precariat working in this sector whose livelihoods are not guaranteed or protected by labour laws. While gig workers' securities have been included in the Code of Social Security, it is yet to be implemented nation-wide. It concludes with a critique of the regulatory regime in India that is supportive of the platform economy but not the security of gig workers.
5 **AI, Machine Learning and Gig Workers in India**: While the focus of the chapter is to explain the nature of algorithmic management using the examples of Swiggy and Uber, it begins by placing AI in the context of the GoI's commitments to AI. The chapter deals with issues around machine learning and automation in a country where there is evidence of underemployment. It also deals with the issue of 'regulatory arbitrage' and the ways in which platforms have used the legislative vacuum to carve out and make a case for the specificities of algorithmic management. The chapter also explores key issues related to the identification and management of populations based on facial recognition technologies (FRTs) – an issue that has bearings on the ways in which delivery and ride-hail platforms manage their workers.
6 **Resistance**: This chapter explores the global development of gig worker resistance and the incipient resistance in India. Based on a conversation with the literature on gig worker resistance, it explores the multifaceted nature of resistance including the establishment of dedicated trade unions, everyday resistance and the role of the State – as in Kerala – providing spaces for alternative, State-owned ride-hail/taxi services. While acknowledging the multifaceted nature of resistance, it makes a case for collective forms of resistance over individual resistance precisely because the former can lead to long-term gains by workers including wages, better working conditions and other securities that rank among the key deficits faced by gig workers.
7 **Cloud, Data Centres and the Politics of Infrastructure**: The platform economy is fundamentally dependent on cloud and data infrastructures. While the GoI has invested in its own cloud initiative – Meghna – both public and private data flows have been captured by Big Tech and, in particular, AWS, Microsoft Azure and others. This reality suggests that the prospects for Made in India and Atmanirbhar Bharat are difficult precisely because of the deep presence of Big Tech in India. The Government of Telangana's policy on data management is highlighted as an example of data management that is explicitly reliant on Big Tech. The chapter highlights the preferential treatment given to cloud and data centre investors, issues with real estate, the skirting of environmental legislations and the long-term consequences of such sops. It includes a conversation with critical infrastructure theory.

8 **AI, Risk and the Gig Economy**: The final chapter deals with the issue of risk in the context of deployments of AI. Unlike the EU that has determined levels of risk, from high to moderate, the GoI has decided that India will be a 'sandbox' for AI experiments across multiple sectors. The chapter deals with risk by having a conversation with Ulrich Beck's theory of Risk and explores the pros and cons of a risk-free/lite approach to AI innovations in India. It particularly deals with how a multistakeholder approach to risk involving civil society can mitigate what can broadly be described as a technocratic turn and the role played by a small group of individuals, NGOs and think tanks in shaping the platformisation of the State and platform policy in India. It makes a case for the regulation of AI that will impact gig workers.

Bibliography

50,000 Aadhar enrolment operators suspended till data: MoS IT (2017), Times of India, December 29. Available at: https://timesofindia.indiatimes.com/business/india-business/50000-aadhaar-enrolment-operators-suspended-till-date-mos-it/articleshow/62296064.cms

Aneja, U. & Chamuah, A. (2020), *A Balancing Act: The promise and peril of Big Tech in India* (1–73), Tandem Research. Available at: https://bigtechinindia.com/Tandem-Research-Big_Tech_report.pdf

Athique, A. & Kumar, A. (2022), Platform ecosystems, market hierarchies and the megacorp: The case of Reliance Jio (1420–1436), *Media, Culture & Society* 44 (8).

Covid database: India's health ministry denies major breach (2023), BBC, June 13. Available at: https://www.bbc.com/news/world-asia-india-65880173

Dreze, J. & Khera, R. (2022), Six types of problems Aadhar is causing – and safeguards needed immediately, Scroll.In, January 2. Available at: https://scroll.in/article/1013700/six-types-of-problems-aadhaar-is-causing-and-safeguards-needed-immediately

Dutta, A., Aditi, A., Ghosal, A., Thomas, A. & Mishra, Y. (2020), Apps, maps and war rooms: on the modes of existence of "COVtech" in India (382–390), *Urban Geography*, 42 (3).

Easterling, K (2014), *Extrastatecraft: The Power of Infrastructure Space*, Verso, London & NY.

Galan, J. I. & Zuniga-Vicente, J. A. (2022), The gig economy: A preliminary proposal of some distinctive forms (1–18) in Ashish Gupta, Tavishi Tewary, Badria Narayanan Gopalakrishnan Eds. *Sustainability in the Gig Economy: Perspectives, Challenges and Opportunities in Industry 4.0*, Springer, Singapore.

Govt allows Aadhar authentication for birth and death registrations (2023), Livemint, The Mint, June 28. Available at: https://www.livemint.com/news/india/govt-allows-aadhaar-authentication-for-birth-and-death-registrations-11687925070068.html

Harvey, D. (2005), *The New Imperialism*, Oxford University Press, Oxford.

Hicks, J. (2020), Digital ID capitalism: how emerging economies are re-inventing digital capitalism (330–350), *Contemporary Politics*, 26 (3).

In the past five year 47 incidents of data leak and 142 data breaches: MeitY, The Wire, March 16. n.d. Available at: https://thewire.in/government/india-data-leak-breach-lok-sabha

Jha, M. K. & Sengupta, R. (2022), *Data Centres as Infrastructure: Frontiers of Digital Governance in Contemporary India*, Orient Blackswan Pvt. Ltd, Hyderabad.

Masiero, S. & Arvidson, V. (2019), Degenerative outcomes of digital identity platforms for development (903–928), Information Systems Journal, 31

Mishra, A. (2017), Ola-Uber drivers to go on strile again, Delhi High Court orders injunction, Inc42, April 17. Available at: https://inc42.com/buzz/ola-uber-sarvodaya-delhihc/
Mishra, R. K. (2019), The Digital State: A tale of tweets and foods in contemporary India (156–171), from Adrian Athique & Emma Baulch (Eds.) *Digital Transactions in India: Economic, informational and social exchanges*, Routledge, NY.
Nair, V. (2019), Governing India in Cybertime: Biometric IDs, Start-Ups and the Temporalised Stare (519–536), *South Asia: Journal of South Asian Studies*, 42 (3).
Raj, K. & Gurmat, S. (2021), As India's gig workers died of Covid-19, their families received neither government nor company aid, Article 14, September 6. Available at: https://article-14.com/post/as-india-s-gig-workers-died-of-covid-19-their-families-receive-neither-govt-nor-company-aid-6135842b68c1a
Rao, U. (2019), Response to 'the Aadhar debate: Where are the sociologists?' (431–440), *Contributions to Indian Sociology*, 53 (3).
Rossiter, N. (2016) *Software, Infrastructure, Labor: A Media Theory of Logistical Nightmares*, Routledge, NY.
Sasikumar, S. K. & Sersia, K. (2020), Digital platform economy: Overvew, emerging trends and policy perspectives (336–347), *Productivity*, 61 (3).
Singh, A. (2021) Big Tech is bending to the Indian Government's will, Wired, August 15. Available at: https://www.wired.com/story/big-tech-is-bending-to-the-indian-governments-will/
StartUpIndia. Available at: https://www.startupindia.gov.in/content/sih/en/international/go-to-market-guide/government-initiatives.html
Thomas, P. N. (2012) *Digital India: Understanding Information, Communication and Social Change*, Sage, New Delhi.
Thomas, P. N. (2019) *The Politics of Digital India: Between Local Compulsions and Transnational Pressures*, Oxford University Press, New Delhi.
Thomas, P. N. (2022), *Information Infrastructures in India*, Oxford University Press, Oxford.
Thomas, P.N. (2023) *Platform Regulation: Exemplars, Approaches and Solutions*, Oxford University Press, Oxford.
Van Dijk, J.,Poell, T. & de Waal, M. (2018), *The Platform Society*, Oxford University Press, NY.
Venkatanarayanan, A. (2017) Aadhar Frauds (Sept.18), Excel Sheet. Available at: https://docs.google.com/spreadsheets/d/1e8aXt6LLMDMcosTzXi0c2Jni3CBW0MYFZBgevu_KZuw/edit#gid=1575209208
Venkatanarayanan, A. (2018), A critical examination of the State of Aadhar report by IDinsight, Medium.com, May 23. Available at: https://medium.com/karana/a-critical-examination-of-the-state-of-aadhaar-2018-report-by-idinsight-ef751e24d6c5
Woodcock, J. & Graham, M. (2020), *The Gig Economy: A Critical Introduction*, Polity, Cambridge/Medford.

Other Resources

Venkatanarayanan, A. (2019), Compromising a $6B big data project through poor data quality: the Aadhar case study. Presented at the The Fifth Elephant 2018 data conference, July 2. Available at: https://hasgeek.com/fifthelephant/2018/sub/compromising-a-6b-big-data-project-through-poor-da-SKtwiSeVG82q4TCrr7KyJF

1 India Stack, Techno-Optimism and Platform Contradictions

What one writes about the 'platform economy' in India is made difficult by the fact that the two words platform and economy on their own and as they relate to India are what may be called unstable signifiers – meaning, that both these words can and often are interpreted, understood and invested with multiple meanings from/in very specific contexts. The result is a semantic overload that is made more complex by the fact that everything that is produced, transacted, distributed and consumed today is attributed to platforms in an economy that have become 'platformised'. There is also a certain ahistoricity about platforms that are only now being addressed. Marc Steinberg (2022), for example, has made a compelling case that traces the lineage of digital platforms to the automobile industry, in particular Toyota's manufacturing processes and production system, the GE to the outsourcing of labour in this industry and data mining to the regulation of production practices at Toyota (1085). This attempt to inflect the platform sublime with its non-digital historical roots is an important corrective to the tendency to narrate a narrow story of origins that often begins with the bursting of the dotcoms bubble in 2008.

It would seem with the benefit of hindsight that we have been here before. Terms, such as knowledge economy and digital economy, are often not historically grounded, are multi-accentual, contested, and complex precisely because their meanings are context-specific. So, coming to an understanding of what constitutes knowledge in a knowledge economy is as complicated as coming to an understanding of the digital economy that is not based on apprehending and accounting for the extraordinary diversity in digital production and digital transactions associated with the informal digital economy. While the GoI is often effusive about employment and opportunities for employment in India, rarely are distinctions made between the formal economy that accounts for ten per cent of employment and the informal economy that accounts for the rest and which has become the space and place for a variety of digital transactions. Such aporias seem to be a characteristic feature of our understandings of issues in our contemporary world. An example of such an aporia is the pervasive 'platform determinism' that is a constitutive feature of the discourse of contemporary digital platforms in India and elsewhere.

DOI: 10.4324/9781003491705-2

India Stack

There is an additional complexity when the words platform and economy become inflected with nationalistic rhetoric and India's ambitions to become a multi-trillion-dollar economy in the not-too-distant future. This ambition is best reflected in the confidence in India's achievements in establishing and deploying the 'India Stack'. The India Stack consists of a family of APIs that enable connectivities between four layers – Presenceless ID authentication via the Aadhar Card (controlled by the Unique Identification Authority of India), Paperless Banking (Department of Electronics and Information Technology), Cashless payments via the UPI (National Payments Corporation of India) and the Consent layer via DigiLocker and other apps that make up a personal data store (Reserve Bank of India) (See India Stack & IBEF). Taken separately or together, the India Stack offers solutions to countries that are keen to enhance digital efficiencies. The software architectures that make up the India Stack are now available as digital public goods through the multi-lateral Digital Public Goods Alliance (Digital Public Goods Alliance). Unlike in the West, where digital capitalism is to a large extent controlled by the private sector and Big Tech, in India, the state has played a primary role in expanding an ID-based digital capitalism. The architecture of India Stack has been created specifically to enable third parties to build apps on top of it thus enabling multiple opportunities for the commercialisation of data.

The confidence in India Stack was on display at the India Stack Developer Conference, on 25 January 2023 organised by the Ministry of Electronics and Information Technology (MeitY) – the objectives of which have been described in wholly altruistic terms – the availability of the open-source, open standards–based digital public goods based on Open API's that are ready to be shared with countries, developers, entrepreneurs and start-ups (https://events.negd.in/). As someone who has both taught and written on open access, open data, open source and the digital commons, I find it intriguing that the GoI has embraced openness and publicly proclaims its intent to contribute to reinstituting the original vision of the internet as a democratic space on the lines articulated by internet pioneers such as Sir Tim Berners Lee. It would seem that the GoI is in the process of establishing its own version of the Information Commons based on universal connectivity and the facilitation of financial inclusivity for its citizens. It is a vision where control over and the use of personal data lies rather emphatically with the government. Arguably this is a top–down, centralised vision with very little space for alternative visions of openness created from below that is in line with the development scripts embraced by successive governments in the post-Independent period. The fact that the GoI has launched 12 national digital projects inclusive of Aadhar (Digital Identity), UPI (Digital Payment), DigiLocker (Paperless Governance) among numerous other nation-scale projects in a country with a 1.3 billion population is an achievement that few countries can match. The scale of these digital rollouts, while extraordinary, is also very ordinary since India does have a reputation for implementing mission-level projects. Such projects, beginning in the early 1950s under the aegis of the Planning Commission (now called NITI Aayog), included nationwide infrastructure development, welfare initiatives and development projects. However, there has always been a question mark over the uneven rollout of these projects, the role played by the bureaucracy and middlemen in limiting development and the long-term impacts of such projects on the average citizen. More problematic is the role played by the corporate sector in the datification and platformisation of India – a project in which they stand to gain the most from public–private partnerships.

On the one hand, this epistemic confidence in home-grown technologies and software solutions is reflective of major achievements in the creation of alternatives to existing platform monopolies and their control over data generated via online search, socialities and commerce. And it is extraordinary that open solutions are becoming the norm after decades of proprietorially conceived, discursive hegemonies. For countries that are keen to invest in efficient forms of e-government, India's open platform architectures are bound to provide adaptable solutions. The delivery of digital services has become an essential aspect of the contract that governments have with their citizens. The India Stack offers countries the opportunity to choose and prioritise layers, to opt for a flexible system in which an individual ID is unnecessary or to invest in such architectures specifically to strengthen governmentality and the power of the state. On the other hand, these software architectures are disconnected from larger social issues such as human rights, privacy and agency. While the description of the India Stack does mention privacy, it does not engage with such issues since the assumption is that citizens trust in the benevolent state that India is. Hence, DigiLocker is celebrated as a wonderfully secure space to keep all of one's digital documents including birth and educational certificates, bank loans, etc. The fact that the RBI is in control of DigiLocker conveys trusthworthiness since the RBI is in charge of India's economy. Yet, it could be the case that this trust in the government is misplaced since they do, in the absence of a national privacy framework, routinely sell data that they have collected to third parties. The Ministry of Road Transport & Highways 'Bulk Data Sharing Policy & Procedure' confirms its sale of data to third parties. Under Section 7 of Cost of Bulk Data subsection (ii), it affirms that 'commercial organizations and individuals seeking bulk data will have to pay an amount of Rs. 3.00 Crore for the FY 2019–20' (Bulk Data Sharing Policy, 3). Kodali (2019) has reported that '87 private entities and 32 government entries' have accessed centralised databases containing millions of vehicle registration and driver license records earning the government 65 crores. In other words, both 'consent' and 'privacy' are circumscribed by government control over and use of data in non-consensual ways. There have also been numerous Aadhar data breaches, with evidence of people selling Aadhar data over WhatsApp and a French data researcher using SQL code injections to hack into Aadhar and obtain account details of 5.6 million Aadhar accounts (Mohan: 2018). Trust in databanks and the security of personal data are among the most contentious and unresolved issues. There are many contenders and platform fiduciaries that include organisations linked to the public and private sectors and civil society.

Over the last two decades, India has become an important player in global supply chains linked to computational, algorithmic productivity, software architectures, digital processing and digital labour. The country also has attempted to create an ambitious project that is directed towards the disruption of traditional economies and its replacement with digital natives involved in a variety of digitally mediated productivities across all sectors including industry, manufacturing and agriculture. The India Stack is the means by which smartphones, authentication and fintech have been welded together to create the digital Indian and the hope is that the impetus from this and public–private partnerships will give a boost to entrepreneurialism, digital innovation and digital solutions in solving the most persistent divides in Indian society. Labour has been clearly affected by the digital mode of production and the new opportunities in employment that have arisen in the context of the digitisation of services. However, it is clear that a fine-grained and textured understanding of the GE remains elusive. The gig platform economy with its diversity of employment opportunities in ride-sharing, food and grocery delivery, cleaning, care and odd jobs (skilled and unskilled) may be considered relatively new given the role played by platforms as intermediaries in flexible employment markets although gig workers also face the very same issues that all workers face – wages, working conditions, benefits – rights, that we often taken for granted for workers in the formal economy. Koutsimpogiorgos, et al. (2020:531) have argued that 'broader definitions of the gig economy are conceivable, including intermediation by offline platforms alongside online platforms, employees alongside independent contractors, unpaid tasks alongside paid tasks, and goods rented out in the sharing economy alongside tasks carried out in the gig economy'.

The Holy Grail of Financial Inclusion

The fact that financial inclusivity is the GoI's key objective is reflected in the space given to fintech in the Indian Stack. Fintech is a moniker used to cover a range of digitally mediated financial services across credit, payments, investment management, personal finance management, bank tech and insurance tech. There are a range of companies involved in fintech ranging from public initiatives such as the UPI to Big Tech such as Google Pay, Amazon Pay and Apple Pay along with literally thousands of smaller companies involved in the technology-based provisionings of financial services. Arguably, their success to some extent has been predicated on their ability to act as data aggregators and mine client-related data in an environment in which the laws related to privacy and consent are either lax or lacking altogether. In this sense, fintech companies have become partners with the government in a large-scale project directed towards transforming every Indian into transactional citizens within data-driven financial markets. It is fascinating to witness the neoliberal impetus in such public–private partnerships that extend to civil society organisations that have been 'astroturfed' by the GoI. While there literally are thousands of stand-alone and competing fintech organisations in India including those that cater to the needs of the precariat, in particular, gig workers (See Chapter 3), Langley & Leyshon (2021:378) in a critical article on fintech make the point that as against the popular notion that fintech 'disintermediates, disrupts and democratises retail money and finances' there are worldwide tendencies towards 'process (es) of reintermediation, consolidation and capitalisation' in this sector – an observation that warrants investigation in the specific context of India.

Platforms, Privacy and Other Shortfalls

Digital financial inclusion as the Holy Grail is widely subscribed to by all those involved in the India Stack. While this project certainly has its merits, taking digital banking to the rural masses simply has to be complemented with the implementation of social policies that help close other divides in society. Digital exceptionalism points to the continuity of a certain way of thinking about the digital divide that stubbornly resists the need for it to be dealt with as just another manifestation of other pre-existing divides in society – gender, caste, class and other markers of identity that continue to define the gaps between the haves and have nots in India. Techno-optimism has played a critical role in the development rhetoric crafted by successive governments ever since the software boom in the 1990s. And this optimism has played an important role in the shaping of techno discourses in India. Today, 'connectivity' is described as a panacea as is 'digital inclusion'. Luke Munn (2022:1412) has made a case for 'epistemic infrastructures' to be taken seriously, the role played by infrastructures in actively producing forms of knowledge that contribute to material effects. Munn assesses the contested nature of infrastructural politics in Hong Kong, in particular, the case of an industrial estate allocating land to a 'data centre rather than a community centre' (1399). Keeping in mind projects such as Digital India and the India Stack and the imperative of achieving efficiencies through connectivity, it is important that we confront the possibility that 'epistemic infrastructures' can 'engender forms of epistemic hegemony' (1412).

India Stack is not the only initiative that is aimed at expanding digital inclusion in India. There are numerous mission-scale projects linked to the creation of access to health, education and employment. However, the gifting of India Stack to the world suggests that India is no longer just a producer of software architectures for its own consumption, but is also confident in handing over source codes and blueprints to governments, technocrats, developers, IT policy-makers and entrepreneurs located anywhere in the world. This perceived large-heartedness certainly contributes to India's international standing and soft diplomacy efforts although it can also be seen as an aspect of an epistemic hegemony that is firmly grounded in techno-solutions to what are intractable socio-economic issues. However, it is telling that this vision is not accompanied by investments in robust measures supportive of data privacy. In fact, the Digital Data Protection Bill that was introduced in late 2022 (after the withdrawal of an earlier avatar, the Personal Data Protection Bill), while unequivocal on measures such as the responsibilities of 'data fiduciaries' and 'data localisation', includes an entire section (8) on 'Deemed Consent' and the compliance of 'Data Principles' to state scrutiny on vaguely described reasons of national security (The DPDPB, 2022). The fact that the GoI's data projects implicitly recognise that any personal data generated via public transactions is owned de facto by the GoI is best illustrated in the Aarogya Setu (Health Bridge) contact-tracing app. App data is hosted by Amazon's Web Services highlighting the fact that public data is routinely stored in private data centres. The fact that this app was developed without any clear frameworks for ensuring privacy and that its impact was limited by smartphone ownership and more prosaic infrastructural deficits such as the lack of electricity and network availability has been highlighted in a chapter by Ranjini Raghavendra (2022:191) in an edited volume *Artificial Intelligence and its Discontents.* The most worrying aspect of AS (Aarogya Setu) is that it there are no limits to the sharing of 'personally identifiable data' with other people, institutions and departments. The fact that the DigiLocker was established before data privacy has become enshrined in law reflects the epistemic priorities that have been hardwired into India's vision of its own digital sublime.

There are other worrying developments in the GoI's relationship with Digital India. India has become the world's leading country in internet shutdowns for the fifth year in a row (BSWebteam) with 84 shutdowns in 2022. Drones have been used extensively by law enforcement agencies to identify protestors even before Drone Rules were established in 2021 (See PIB) –for example, protestors against the Citizen Amendment Act (CAA) (2019). It is also a country that is at the forefront of experimenting with surveillance (the home secretary approves 7,500–9,000 interceptions every month, Deep:2023), that includes, under its ambit, non-government organisations (NGOs) that receive funds from abroad. The Ministry of Home Affairs has established a centralised monitoring system – a central data hub specifically to monitor NGOs who will be given a unique identity number akin to Aadhar. While the official reason given for this hub is the need to monitor funds used for terror and 'anti-India activities', the term anti-India is typically used by the incumbent government to describe any organisation that questions the country's human rights record or highlights state-sponsored human rights violations (Mukherjee:2023a). The latter was graphically and rather publicly illustrated by the government's banning of the BBC's two-part documentary on the Gujarat riots followed by a 'tax raid' on BBC offices in New Delhi (Frayer: 2023).

The gap between development policy and practice was demonstrated most graphically during mobilisations related to the Right to Information movement (1990–2005). Transparency and accountability audits conducted on development expenditures throughout the country unearthed many corrupt practices including the siphoning of public money by all levels of personnel working in the government development machinery (See Mander and Joshi:n.d.). Akhil Gupta's (2012) classic study on the structural violence of an uncaring, indifferent bureaucracy highlights the reality of corruption by other means, the arbitrary nature of care and its consequences for the poor in the context of neoliberal economic growth in the North Indian state of Uttar Pradesh. Gupta's rather sobering analysis attempts to go beyond the rhetoric of development and deal with its reality – the messy nature of project implementation and the extra-development factors that have contributed to a stymieing of development outcomes in India. I think that India's love affair with all things digital needs to be similarly contextually assessed by independent researchers in order to understand the practical difference this has made to the lives of ordinary people. Direct Benefit Transfers based on bank accounts, Aadhar cards and mobile phones (known as JAM: Jan Dhan, Aadhar, Mobile) may contribute to the cashless society although the substitution of cash for in-kind welfare entitlements (Sen:2013) and the 32 per cent slashing of the budget of the Mahatma Gandhi National Rural Employment Guarantee Act in 2023 to Rs. 60,000 crore (a scheme that made up 80 per cent of income loss during the Covid pandemic) (Sen:2023) indicate serious shortfalls in the provisioning of welfare even as India transforms into a multi-trillion-dollar economy.

Keith Breckenridge's (2019:104) writings on biometrics in South Africa have dealt with many issues related to the security of data but also with the politics of the private company Net1 that was involved through its South African subsidiary Cash Paymaster Services in disbursing welfare subsidies to South Africa's poor. As he has observed, in that process

> the company built up a set of products on the smart cards themselves that offered merchants, lenders and large employers irresistible tools for managing their monetary relationships with the poor, with each other, and with the large banks. These latter transactions for life-insurance, loans, air-time, and prepaid electricity provided a rich and vaguely legal field of opportunity to reward politically connected rent-seekers who sold on commission

at the expense of their customers most of whom belong to South Africa's poor. There are lessons here for India Stack given its control over literally billions of online transactions conducted in an environment that is being shaped and run through public–private partnerships.

The NITI Aayog Report on India's Booming Gig and Platform Economy

The GoI's techno-optimism is best illustrated in the 124-page report from NITI Aayog – *India's Booming Gig and Platform Economy: Perspective and Recommendations on the Future of Work* (2022). With separate chapters on the gig workforce in India, technology diffusion and democratisation of jobs, digital economy and social inclusion and issues with the GE and social security, the report paints an extraordinarily optimistic picture of digital workers and those in the non-digital economy in the informal sector. There are many assumptions in this text that reflect what is the core idea in platform capitalism – anyone armed with a mobile phone has the potential to exploit low entry barriers, enjoy the benefits from work reliability (the availability of gigs), earn better incomes and experience occupational mobility (xix). This way of thinking reminded me of the theorist of Modernisation, Walt Rostow (1959), who had a very mechanical and linear understanding of the stages of economic growth. All countries had to go through these five steps – traditional society, preconditions for take-off, take-off, drive to maturity and age of high mass consumption to become modern. The market, manufacturing and industrialisation were the pre-conditions for growth, productivity and a modern economy. Rostow's stages are context-lite in the sense that they do not factor in the reality of diversity and variety in political economies much like the NITI Aayog report that does not factor in all the extra-platform factors that can and do play a significant role in shaping the quality of employment in the GE. The government's investments in connectivity and financial inclusion via its India Stack adds to the overall quality of life for all workers in the GE in India. As the report claims 'Platform workers enjoy flexibility and choice of labour, ability to hold multiple jobs, guaranteed payments, augmentation of assets, heightened earnings, etc. In a platform economy, individuals merely armed with an internet-enabled smartphone and an asset – such as the tangible vehicle...or intangible skill of cooking or plumbing – can monetise their assets to become platform workers' (29). While there certainly has been an exponential increase of workers in the GE in India – 15 million in 2021 expected to grow to 23.5 million in 2025 (these figures vary and often include workers in the informal economy), there is very little platform sector-specific data on these numbers. While traditional workers in manufacturing, industry and agriculture are covered by labour laws and can belong to unions and enjoy rights, the same cannot be said for workers in the GE. In an effort to modernise its labour laws, the GoI consolidated 29 national-level labour laws into four codes – Code on Wages (enacted 2019), Industrial Relations Code (Enacted 2020), the Code on Social Security (Enacted 2020) and the Occupational Safety, Health and Working Conditions Code (Enacted 2020) (See the National Law Review). However, with the exception of the Code on Social Security, there is a conspicuous absence of considerations given to gig workers in the other Codes. Chapter IX – Social Security of Unorganised Workers, Gig Workers and Platform Workers explicitly includes the intent of the central government to frame schemes specifically related to the welfare of gig and platform workers in Section 114 (1) including '(a) life and disability cover; (b) accident insurance; (c) health and maternity benefits; (d) old age protection; (e) crèche; and (f) any other benefit as may be determined by the Central Government' (69). Aggregators (platform intermediaries) would need to contribute to these schemes. It is envisaged that social security will be funnelled through the Employees Provident Fund Organisation, Employees State Insurance Corporation and a Social Security Fund that aggregators will be required to contribute towards. While this is a welcoming development, the fact that the three other Codes have failed to include legal provisions with respect to wages, occupational health and safety and working conditions for gig workers is indicative of the government's piecemeal approach to dealing with one of the fastest growing sectors for employment in India. There has however been a lack of urgency and this law is yet to come into force contributing to gig worker insecurities (Mohanty:2023). While the report from NITI Aayog does include sections on the welfare of gig workers, the overall emphasis is on employment opportunities and the dividends that the Indian economy will earn from GE. In the words of Islam and Kain (2022) "The report uses the word 'potential' 66 times and the word 'growth' 93 times, accurately indicating the general upbeat tone adopted towards the gig and platform economy in popular discourse. In contrast, the words 'protest', 'strike', 'unions', and 'workers' associations' find no mention despite a significant and growing gig workers' movement, which has led to the emergence of new unions such as the All India Gig Workers' Union, Indian Federation of App-Based Transport Workers, and the Telangana Gig and Platform Workers' Union".

Growth in the Context of Alternative Statistics

One of the more pressing issues facing the Indian economy is the lack of reliable data on economic indices and the use of compromised data to build an image of an ascendant superpower and economic powerhouse. This attempt to create a counternarrative of growth and prosperity has been especially evident in the post-2014 era of rule by the BJP and its brand of Hindu nationalism. Economist Jayati Ghosh (2020), in an article in the *South Asia Multidisciplinary Academic Journal*, has highlighted the ways in which prominent, internationally acclaimed institutions involved in the collection of statistical data in India including the National Statistical Commission, the Central Statistical Organisation and the National Sample Survey Organisation have become politicised and now exclusively report 'positive' news on unemployment, nutrition intake and so on. Ghosh specifically deals with the manipulation of the measurements of GDP. In her words,

> 'One significant change was the shift from using the Index of Industrial Production (a real measure of output) as one of the primary indicators of industrial GDP to using data from company reports compiled by the Ministry of Corporate Affairs. That database is seriously flawed: with a significant proportion (around one-third) of dummy companies, it shows very wide fluctuations; and is likely to reflect incentives for companies to misstate their returns, especially in quick estimates'
>
> (4)

As reported in the *Financial Express* newspaper, in 2019, 108 economists and social scientists in India wrote a signed letter to the government expressing their concern with the manipulation of official statistics (Jain:2019, Bradsher:2019. See also Kumar, et al.:2020). Company reports submitted to the Securities and Exchange Board of India (SEBI) are not scrutinised to the extent that they should be and it often takes a major scam such as the Hindenburg Report (2023) into stock manipulations at the Adani Group that led to the inflated valuations of this group for evidence related to India's 'real' economic growth to become public. In fact, SEBI's footdragging related to the Hindenburg Report and its perceived lack of interest in investigating the substantive questions over the probity of the Adani group raised in the Hindenburg Report has been questioned by the former Director of the Reserve Bank of India, Raghuram Rajan (Mukherjee:2023b). Rukmini (2022), in an article in the *Quint*, highlights the Modi government's refusal in 2019 to release the CES conducted by the National Statistical Office in 2017–2018 because it revealed declines in real income levels – a case of an intentional delay in the making of less-than-flattering data on the government's economic performance public. In response, and under the aegis of the NITI Aayog, there has been an attempt to create an alternative set of development indexes to score and rank states and districts in India in line with the GoI's aspiration to transform India into an economic superpower. These include the Aspirational Districts Programme, the Sustainable Development Goals Index, the Agriculture Transformation Index, the India Innovations Index and the Composite Water Management Index. As Samdub (2022) describes it, these indexes are 'Equal parts expert calculation and public relations apparatus, these indices are dramatized in publicly accessible dashboards, policy briefs, press reports, and social media posts. In spite of their supporters' claims, indices are far from neutral, transparent, or objective measures of performance. 1 Rather, by pitting administrative units against each other, they render development as competition, centralizing state power and promoting entrepreneurship as the answer to poverty'.

This rather flippant attitude towards public data is also replicated in the private sector. Having assessed company reports of groups such as Reliance that have substantial interests in the telecom sector myself, I can vouch for the serious limitations that exist in the quality of data on telecom subscriptions that are often aggregated and not available per sector.

Key Characteristics of India's Digital Economy

So what are some of the characteristics of India's economy and digital economy from the perspective of critical political economy?

1 India's ability to establish multi-sectoral national digital projects linked to connectivity is proven. There is expertise in the creation of software architectures, thriving public–private partnerships, and national digital research

labs along with the political will to transform India into a digital nation. India Stack is one example of the numerous achievements in the digital space.

2 This vision of the digital sublime is however abstracted from citizen concerns including data privacy, surveillance, ad hoc and restrictive regulatory rulings and the expansion of control over transactional data by the State.

3 The overall trajectory of development in India is a type of neoliberalism that is accompanied by populist nationalism that is inclined towards the exertion of control. While the State favours public–private partnerships and the involvement of the corporate sector, it has also expressed its interest in withdrawing selectively from state involvement in development – as for instance, the promulgation of three farm laws (The Farmers' Produce Trade and Commerce (Promotion and Facilitation) Bill, 2020 and The Farmers (Empowerment and Protection) Agreement of Price Assurance and Farm Services Bill, 2020) that would have led to the privatisation of agriculture and to the exertion of market control over production, pricing, procurement and consumption with serious consequences for the PDS and subsidised distribution of essential grain and oils. Cutting subsidies to the NREGA in 2023 is another example of State withdrawal from its involvement in welfare.

4 However, this withdrawal simply has to be selective as the substitution of cash welfare payments in a cashless society (an avowed ambition of the present government) in place of in-kind entitlements is a risky proposition given the precarity of and volatility in buying essentials in the open market unmoored from price guarantees.

5 While the regulatory moment has arrived in India, the focus for regulation is Big Tech. Arguably, the regulation of platforms is required precisely because these large multinational platforms have been able to make a case for 'platform exceptionalism' and evade regulatory scrutiny at a variety of levels. The Equalisation Levy – India's answer to Google Tax, Information Technology (Intermediary Guidelines and Digital Media Ethics Code) Rules 2021 to regulate OTT platforms, the proposed Digital India Act, the proposed law on Digital Competition, Cryptocurrency and Regulation of Official Digital Currency Bill, 2021 ('draft Bill'), The Data Protection Bill and the Open Network for Digital Commerce (ONDC) are some of the policies that are specifically directed towards creating a level playing field in India after what has been a regulatory vacuum that the world's major digital platforms exploited for two decades. The ONDC is meant to contest the dominance of Amazon and Flipkart – an entirely laudable project – and enable local family businesses (*kiranas*) to compete with the big e-commerce player on an equal footing. However, despite the importance of these regulatory measures, the influence of Big Tech in India as data aggregators and data controllers is extensive. So while regulation affects some parts of Amazon – notably its retail and streaming services – its role as the leading provider of cloud services in India is largely unregulated given that there is no specific regulation of cloud services in the country. In the absence of

specific legislations, there are the Reserve Bank of India's guidelines on Managing Risk and Code of Conduct in Outsourcing of Financial Services by Banks, the IT Act and Privacy Rules and the Insurance Regulatory and Development Authority of India's Guidelines on Information and Cyber Security for Insurers although these are indirect regulatory mechanisms (Chengappa & Mathur:2019). The fact remains that both the central and state governments in India are heavily reliant on the data services provided by Amazon, Google, Microsoft and other Big Tech. At the same time, there has been an attempt to take over regulatory bodies involved in overseeing development, the market, the media and the judiciary including NITI Aayog, the Telecom Regulatory Authority of India, the Securities and Exchange Board of India and even the Supreme Court.

6 Even India's famously independent media have more or less been brought under government control through government withdrawal of public advertising from erring newspapers and through indirect control such as the take-over of the only independent news channel, NDTV, by a favoured corporate, the Adanis in late 2022.

7 What these changes point to is the Indian State's attempt to establish an institutional framework for reform that offers a new type of distributive politics that favours corporates, in particular, corporates that are deeply involved in public–private partnerships such as the Ambanis and Adanis. Kashwan et al. (2019), in an article on the relationship between power and neoliberalism, make a distinction between two forms of power – 'power over' and 'power to' 'For us the key difference between 'power over' and 'power to' resides in whether power is exerted by constraining of the opportunities and control that actors and agencies previously had (power over), or by creating new opportunities – i.e. new resources, structures and institutions – and relatively greater control than individuals and groups of individuals enjoyed previously (power to). 'Power to' thus includes resistance and empowerment, as well as learning and cooperation, which can lead to defense/reinforcement of existing institutions, or to institutional innovations or transformations'. Given the GoI's investments in curbing and controlling the power of civil society, both 'power over' and 'power to' have become, more or less, prerogatives of the State.

8 Aiwha Ong (2006), in her study *Neoliberalism as Exception*, refers to the meaning of 'exception' as the power to both include and exclude a strategy in which some groups become a target for 'calculative choices and value-orientation' (5). She makes a case to explore both neoliberalism as an exception and exception to liberalism as the basis for understanding the specificity of forms that neoliberalism takes. In the specific case of India, market-based economic growth is accompanied by a Hindu nationalist ideology that extolls majoritarian economic, cultural, political and social growth (the exception) and their setting apart at the expense of minorities who are often described as not fully Indian and who are increasingly being denied their rights to moral claims and values in a secular country. This publicly

articulated discourse of populist nationalism and Hindu exceptionalism is often invoked during pre-electoral rallies organised by the BJP and its allies. The anti-constitutional and anti-secular nature of a discourse that has become normalised, in turn, provides a framework for minority group assessments of digital India and is the basis for real and imaginary concerns with the government's digital intent and the spectre of dystopian, disquieting futures linked to platform governmentalities.

9 So the platform economy in India is grounded in an authoritarian neoliberalism and in a context in which key institutions involved in social policymaking across sectors are being brought under the control of the government in power. This is a deliberate process that is often invisible but that occasionally becomes public when the media report on history textbooks for school children being rewritten to erase India's Mughal past or extol the virtues of Hindu demagogues at the expense of freedom fighters or when stories of India's civilisational achievements are cited from scriptures to highlight India's ancient prowess in science and technology. While such developments may not, on the face of it, have any bearings on the GE or platform regulation, this is a parallel development that does have material effects on the story of cashless India. From a critical political economy perspective, both stories are important and even if the story of social engineering is not going to be foregrounded in this volume, its long shadow needs to be acknowledged. The same communities who face internet shutdowns are often those who face other devaluations – social, cultural, political and economic. Muslim and Dalit food delivery workers have faced the ire of anti-Muslim and anti-Dalit customers. Naraharisetty (2022), in the online news service *The Swaddle*, narrates the stories of two Muslim gig workers in Hyderabad – Ahmed working for Swiggy who was on the job when he got delivery instructions that explicitly said 'Please only allow Hindu delivery person' and Saleem, an Uber driver who was on his way to a pickup a customer when he was waylaid, beaten up and the car burnt by Hindu extremists. 'The problem begins with the fact that platform apps are legally not liable to protect their workers. And thus, protections for gig workers remain abysmally low. … But the incidents point to a new form of worker vulnerability that conversations about gig work haven't yet caught up with: bigotry and safety from violence. Both incidents on Swiggy and Uber took place while workers were on the job and logged into the platform to complete a service. But in both instances, neither platform felt any responsibility toward the workers' safety. There are several ways platforms can make working conditions safer and protected from discrimination, but it all boils down to how there's no incentive to do so' (Naraharisetty:2022). Neither the State nor these platforms are willing to deal with the rights of gig workers. When there is normalisation of bigotry, there are no limits to the spaces and places for enactments of discrimination.

Bibliography

Adani Group: How the World's 3rd Richest Man Is pulling the Largest Con in Corporate History Hindenburg Research (January 24 2023). Available at: https://hindenburgresearch.com/adani/

Bradsher, K. (2019), yes, India's Economy Is Growing But Can You Trust the Data? *New York Times*, May 30. Available at: https://www.nytimes.com/2019/05/30/business/india-economy.html

Breckenridge, K. (2019), The Global Ambitions of the Biometric Anti-Bank: Net1 Lockin and the Technologies of African Financialisation (93–118), *International Review of Applied Economics*, 33 (1).

BSWebTeam, With 84 Internet Shutdowns in 2022, India Tops the List Fifth Time in a Row (2023), *Business Standard*, February 28. Available at: https://www.business-standard.com/article/current-affairs/with-84-internet-shutdowns-in-2022-india-tops-the-list-fifth-time-in-a-row-123022800281_1.html

Bulk Data Sharing Policy (2019) 1–5. Available at: https://parivahan.gov.in/parivahan/sites/default/files/NOTIFICATION%26ADVISORY/8March%202019.pdf

Chengappa, M. and Mathur (no initials), (2019), Snapshot: Cloud Computing Regulation in India, *Lexology*, November 18. Available at: https://www.lexology.com/library/detail.aspx?g=cd257198-8021-425c-a5ca-4df7a8a93997

Deep, A. (2023), NGO's Flag 'Generalised Surveillance' of Citizens in Delhi High Court, *The Hindu*, January 19. Available at: https://www.thehindu.com/sci-tech/technology/ngos-flag-generalised-surveillance-of-citizens-in-delhi-high-court/article66408253.ece

Digital Public Goods Alliance. Available at: https://digitalpublicgoods.net/who-we-are/

Drone Rules, 2021. Press Information Bureau, January 28, 2022. Available at: https://static.pib.gov.in/WriteReadData/specificdocs/documents/2022/jan/doc202212810701.pdf

Frayer, L. (2023), Indian Tax Inspectors Leave BBC Offices After Nearly 60 Hours of Questioning, *NPR*, February 16. Available at: https://www.npr.org/2023/02/16/1157428195/bbc-india-raid-modi

Ghosh, J. (2020), Hindutva, Economic Neoliberalism and the Abuse of Economic Statistics in India (1–8), *South Asia Multidisciplinary Academic Journal*, 24/25. Available at: https://journals.openedition.org/samaj/6882

Gupta, A. (2012), *Red Tape: Bureaucracy, Structural Violence, and Poverty in India*, Orient BlackSwan, Hyderabad.

India Consolidates and Codifies its National Level Labour Laws (2023), The National Law Review, XIII(63).

India Stack, https://indiastack.org/

India's Booming Gig and Platform Economy: Perspectives and Recommendations on the Future of Work (2022) (1–124), NITI Aayog, June, Sansad Marg, New Delhi.

Indian Brand Equity Foundation (IBEF), A Public Digital Infrastructure: India Stack. Available at: https://www.ibef.org/blogs/a-public-digital-infrastructure-india-stack

Indian Stack Developer's Conference, (January 22–23, 2022). Available at: https://events.negd.in/

Islam, A. and Kain, D. (2022), Perils of the Gig Economy, *The India Forum*, October 25. Available at: https://www.theindiaforum.in/forum/perils-gig-economy

Jain, S. (2019), If Modi Is Accused of manipulating GDP Data, He Has Only Himself to Blame, *The Financial Express*, March 15. Available at: https://www.financialexpress.com/opinion/if-modi-is-accused-of-manipulating-gdp-data-he-has-only-himself-to-blame/1517569/

Kashwan, P., MacLean, L. M. and Garcia-Lopez, G. A. (2019), Rethinking Power and Institutions in the Shadows of Neoliberalism (An introduction to a Special Issue of World Development) (133–146), *World Development*, 120.
Kodali, S. (2019), The Dangers that Lurk Within India's Vision of Becoming a Data Republic, *The Wire*, July 12. Available at: https://thewire.in/government/india-vision-data-republic-dangers-privacy
Koutsimpogiorgos, N., van Slagaren, J., Herrmann, A. M. and Frenken, K. (2020), Conceptualising the Gig Economy and Its Regulatory Problems (525–545), *Policy & Internet*, 12 (4).
Kumar, A., Mohanan, P. C. and Kundu, A. (2020), Disastrous decade for data: The way forward (18–21), *Economic & Political Weekly*, LV(41).
Langley, P. and Leyshon, A. (2021), The Platform Political Economy of FINTECH: Reintermediation, Consolidation and Capitalisation (376–388), *New Political Economy*, 26 (3).
Mander, H. and Joshi, A. The Movement for Right to Information in India: People's Power for the Control of Corruption (1–46). Available at: https://www.humanrightsinitiative.org/programs/ai/rti/india/articles/The%20Movement%20for%20RTI%20in%20India.pdf
Mohan, D. (2018), What Is the Indian Stack and Why Is It No Longer the Dream It Used to Be (2018), *Fintech Futures*, March 26. Available at: https://www.fintechfutures.com/2018/03/what-is-the-india-stack-and-why-is-it-no-longer-the-dream-it-used-to-be/
Mohanty, B. K. (2023), Govt Vague on Gig Worker Security, *The Telegraph Online*, March 4. Available at: https://www.telegraphindia.com/india/govt-vague-on-gig-worker-security/cid/1914193
Mukherjee, A. (2023a), Surveillance & Clampdown: 'NGOs to Be Linked to Central Data Hub with Unique ID', *The New Indian Express*, March 2. Available at: https://www.newindianexpress.com/nation/2023/mar/02/surveillance--clampdown-ngos-to-be-linked-to-central-data-hub-with-unique-id-2552166.html
Mukherjee, S. (2023b), Adani Row: Why Sebi Didn't Get to Bottom of Issues Raised by Hindenburg Asks Raghuram Rajan, *Mint*, March 5. Available at: https://www.livemint.com/companies/news/adani-row-why-sebi-didn-t-get-to-bottom-of-issues-raised-by-hindenburg-asks-raghuram-rajan-11678024190946.html
Munn, L. (2022), Thinking Through Silicon: Cables and Servers as Epistemic Infrastructures (1399–1416), *New Media & Society*, 24 (6).
Naraharisetty, R. (2022), Muslim Gig Workers Are Beginning to Face Bigotry on the Job – And Nobody Is Helping, *The Swaddle*, October 19. Available at: https://theswaddle.com/muslim-gig-workers-are-beginning-to-face-bigotry-on-the-job-and-nobody-is-helping/
Ong, A. (2006), *Neoliberalism as Exception: Mutations in Citizenship and Sovereignty*, Duke University Press, Durham.
Raghavendra, R. C. (2022), Controversial Covid-19 Contact-Tracing App in India: Digital Self-Defence, Governance and Surveillance (179–196), in A. Hanemaayer (ed.), *Artificial Intelligence and its Discontents: Critiques from the Social Sciences and the Humanities, Social and Cultural Studies of Robots and AI*, Palgrave Macmillan, Cham.
Rostow, W. (1959), The Stage of Economic Growth (1–16), *The Economic History Review*, New Series, 12 (1).
Rukmini, S. (2022), India, Once a Trailblazer in Data Infrastructure, Is Squandering Its Legacy, *The Quint*, July 1. Available at: https://www.thequint.com/opinion/india-once-a-trailblazer-in-data-infrastructure-is-squandering-its-legacy#read-more
Samdub, M. (2022), Governance Interface: The Index in Modi's India (473–493), *Public Culture*, 34 (3).

Sen, H. A. (2013) *Direct Benefits Transfer: Cash vs In-Kind*, Yojana, February. Available at:http://insightsonindia.com/wp-content/uploads/2013/09/dbt-critical-yojana-february-2013.pdf

Sen, J. (2023) Chart: Budget 2023's NREGA Allocation Is Lower than all Previous Modi 2.0 Years, *The Wire*. February 1. Available at: https://thewire.in/economy/nrega-budget-allocation-2023-24

Steinberg, M. (2022), From Automobile Capitalism to Platform Capitalism: Toyotism as a Prehistory of Digital Platform (1069–1090), *Organisation Studies*, 43 (7).

The Code on Social Security, 2020 (1–116) Ministry of Law and Justice. The Gazette of India, September 28. Available at: https://labour.gov.in/sites/default/files/SS_Code_Gazette.pdf

The Digital Personal Data Protection Bill (1–24), 2022. Available at: https://www.meity.gov.in/writereaddata/files/The%20Digital%20Personal%20Data%20Potection%20Bill%2C%202022_0.pdf

Other References

Ep.6: Financial inclusion, privacy and the Indian Stack model, Jack of all Trades. Available at: https://podcasts.apple.com/us/podcast/ep-06-financial-regulation-privacy-the-india-stack-model/id1518307761?i=1000508381166

2 The Governance/Mis-Governance of Start-Ups

Two events in 2023, the Hindenburg Report on the Adani group of companies and the rapid unravelling of India's most valuable ed-tech start-up Byju's that was valued at $22 billion in 2022 have brought issues such as regulation, corporate governance or the lack of it, state complicity and the culture of fast growth and quick returns expected by venture capitalists into sharp focus. Both the Adani group and Byju's grew rapidly in the space of a few years enabled by mergers and acquisitions. Byju's for example spent $2.1 billion in 2021 in its acquisition of ed-tech firms Whitehat Jr, Aakash, Toppr, Epic and Great Learning (Sebastian:2023). Byju's biggest investor and shareholder Prosus NV downgraded its valuation to $5.1 billion in 2022 after evidence of unpaid loans, inflated revenues, lack of financial reporting and layoffs of over 25,000 staff. Adani's market capitalisation has come down to $98 billion in 2023 from $138 billion in 2022. While there is a system of rules, practices and processes that govern the corporate sector and that is intended to contribute towards trust for investors, creditors and other stakeholders, rules that in the case of Adani were bent by the intervention of political capital, this structure has largely provided a framework for the functioning, accountability and transparency of corporate governance in India. Start-ups though have been exempted from needing to abide by governance mechanisms including reporting, accounting and compliance and instead have largely been left to self-regulate. As a result, the Registrar of Companies in India does not have an accurate figure related to the number of start-ups in India (See Sureban:2023). In the case of Adani, while a Supreme Court–established committee did investigate the role of the stock market regulator Securities and Exchange Board of India (SEBI), it has largely exonerated both SEBI and Adani. Questions however remain. Arun Kumar (2023) writing in *The Wire* has raised three questions – "first, how did Adani get hold of so many businesses so quickly? Second, how did the valuation of the shares of the Adani Group rise so rapidly? Third, why did the undue rise in the share prices not raise suspicions among the regulatory agencies – SEBI, the Enforcement Directorate, income tax department, etc.? Did political connections coupled with a lack of action, or investigation by the regulators help Adani acquire assets, possibly at low prices?"

DOI: 10.4324/9781003491705-3

Financialisation and The Start-Up State

Both examples highlight regulatory lapses in a context in which economic growth and ambitions to be a market leader have taken priority at the expense of robust regulatory requirements and the long-term credibility of the increasingly data-driven market economy in India. This economy is being driven by the State investing in the start-up ecosystem and online financial architectures such as the UPI in conjunction with investments made by venture capitals. The objective of this exercise is to establish a new infrastructure in India based on the fusion between the digital and finance – what Jain & Gabor (2020:816) have described as 'digital financialisation'. In this scenario, the State provides all the necessary backend support, including the re-purposing of financial instruments and institutions, architectures such as India Stack, policy, incentives including tax breaks and radical initiatives such as de-monetisation in return for significant, predominantly external financial investments. In other words, State commitment both paves the way for increasing financialisation and mitigates the risk associated with investments by private capital in ventures that may or may not be successful. Traditional analogue banks that the majority of Indians rely on for financial security have been forced to become nimble and support rather than resist the emergence of this new, competitive, data-based, financial market. Having said that the Reserve Bank of India (RBI) is committed to regulating Fintech and ensuring that the products and services that they offer such as pre-paid payment instruments (PPIs) and on-demand loans are not mediated through the UPI interface – thereby ensuring the accountability, trust and security that is in-built into the regulated bank loan credit system is kept distinct from Fintech credit that is easier to access but that belongs to an unregulated market. The RBI's commitment to prudent monetary and fiscal policies and its cautious approach can and does occasionally clash with the GoI's advancement of financial innovation in its avatar as a promotor of state financialisation. Karwowski (2019:1002) defines state financialisation in terms of the state's "adoption of financial logics, advancing financial innovation" by creating "new financial instruments and markets, embracing financial accumulation strategies and financialising the lives of citizens". The fulfilment of these four objectives has been the key priority of the Indian state. This has led to technocratic and financial elites playing an increasingly important role in governance decisions, an issue that has been explored in Chapter 8. There is a sense in which the 'demonetisation' of Rs 500 and 1000 notes on 8 November 2016 that led to a sharp decline in the availability of hard cash and was described as an initiative that was aimed at curbing money laundering actually helped accelerate financial transactions, digital payments and the transactional economy in India (See Adil & Hatekar:2020). What the State guarantees in digital financial markets is the ability of start-ups to collect and monetise data based on the national rollout of payment interfaces such as the UPI irrespective of Acts such as the Digital Personal Data Protection Act, 2023 (DPDPA) that are focussed on curbing and controlling Big Tech as significant data fiduciaries. In fact, India is keen to be described as a Start-Up Nation. January 16 of every year is celebrated as the National Start-Up Day as this was the day when the Start-Up India policy was established in 2016. The GoI's commitment to this initiative is also reflected in its establishment of the StartUp-2 Engagement Group that is a key part of India's presidency of the G20 (Subramaniam:2023). It is estimated that there are close to 55,000 start-ups in India, the third largest start-up ecosystem employing 1.5 million people and worth $350 billion (Pai & Baid:2021). However, the venture capital that sustains start-ups tends to be concentrated in six key cities – with 86 per cent of the capital concentrated in Delhi, Bengaluru and Mumbai. Out of the 123 government-recognised incubators, more than half of these are in key cities that have the infrastructure, established technology institutions and supply of skilled labour (Rault & Mathew:2019:48–49). The start-up nation also known as the start-up state is highly aspirational since it is reflective of a clear break from India's top-heavy, highly bureaucratic, approach to development characterised by five-year plans and the old planning commission. The start-up nation embraces private capital's involvement in the building of Digital India highlighted in NITI Aayog's approach towards the gig economy and gig labour. Vijayanka Nair (2019:523), in an article on the re-imagination of the state in India as a start-up state, reflects on the tendency of technocrats and others involved in the re-imagination to describe all national mission–level projects such as the Aadhar/UIDAI in the language of start-ups.

> I suggest that Aadhaar is the emblematic project of the state reconfigured as what I will call the 'start-up state'. Neither fully state, nor fully start-up, the start-up state is (in) a state of becoming. In using the term 'start-up state', I am pointing to three things. One, that as a platform for start-ups, the start-up state integrates an *ab initio* and largely technological approach to socioeconomic problems. This would-be state is unencumbered by the pedantry and proceduralism of the post-colonial state. Two, that every time a start-up melds with the state, the fusing configures the state as an entity born anew. Even as Aadhaar architects were careful to maintain that a start-up must reintegrate into government, officials keenly communicated to me that Aadhaar, revolutionary as it was, could 'completely transform' the state. It is plausible to suggest, then, that the start-up state is a state permanently *in potentia*. As it encounters challenges, the state forges start-ups, which in turn regenerate the state; the process continues ad infinitum. My last observation is that the state is increasingly appealing to, and becoming the venue for, a start-up approach to 'grand challenges' that banks on the genius of a few (recruited from any sector) to give direction to the competence of many (in the government).

Nair's observations are important not least because the GoI's approach to start-ups, creating an enabling environment, financial support and the nurturing of start-ups, stands in stark contrast to its approach to the welfare of gig workers who have been left to the mercy of pioneering start-ups such as Swiggy and Uber. While there is certainly merit in inviting private capital to deal with some of the grand challenges facing the nation, a complete belief in technocratic solutions simply is not sustainable given the real socio-economic and other challenges faced by the citizens of India for whom connected efficiencies simply are not a substitute for access to basic needs that are key to their survival as individuals and members of a community.

While it is important that Byju's takes responsibility for the mess that it finds itself in, I think some of the blame should be placed on venture capitalists like Prosus and accounting firms such as Deloitte who contribute to the culture of start-ups and who in this case decided to exit from Byju's only after it became apparent that it had multiple issues in the areas of governance, financial accountability, staff lay-offs, strategic, operational and legal issues. As Chakraborty (2023) writing in NikkeiAsia has observed

> VC firms were anxious to grab a piece of the Indian action, pouring $6.4 billion into Indian edtechs in 2020 and 2021, more than four times as much as in the previous two years. Seventy-five institutions invested in Byju's, including Bond Capital, General Atlantic, Lightspeed Venture Partners, the Qatar Investment Authority and International Finance Corporation.

There were 6,639 education start-ups in India in 2023 more than the total number in the UK and the USA. Arguably, both the governance structures and ecosystems that support start-ups in India need to be better regulated. The fact that a representative from the start-up GoMechanic on Byju's board, a company that itself was under investigation for financial irregularities and laid off 70 per cent of its own staff, had stepped down suggests the deep-rooted nature of the challenges facing the governance of start-ups in India (Jain & Jain:2023).

Privacy, The Digital Personal Data Protection Act and Start-Ups

One of the major issues facing Indian citizens today is the security of personal data that has the potential to be compromised by less-than-secure national data storage systems and the GoI's final authority over personal data, its sale to third parties and in particular to corporates. This issue of personal data and who has ultimate control over personal data has been foregrounded in light of the DPDPA that was passed in 2023. It would seem that the responsibility of start-ups over how they use personal data is less of a concern than Big Tech's responsibilities given their descriptor as significant data fiduciaries.

The Digital Personal Data Protection Bill, 2023 (DPDPB) was passed by both the lower and upper houses of parliament in India and was assented to by the president on 11 August to become the DPDPA. It replaced the Personal Data Protection Bill that was introduced in the Parliament in 2018 and withdrawn in 2022 after criticisms from industry. A Joint Select Committee was constituted to revise this bill in light of its perceived shortcomings. While it is absolutely critical that Big Tech have been brought under a consent framework that will govern how they deal with personal transactional data, it would seem that the DPDPA, like its previous avatar, has taken it for granted that the GoI and various entities linked to the GoI will have carte blanche control over all personal data generated and transacted over platforms, ostensibly in the interests of national security. This is clearly expressed in the section Chapter IV Special Provisions (11–12) in the DPDPA 17(1, clauses a–f) where GoI-related entities do not have to negotiate consent when access to personal information is deemed necessary to the interests of national security and in the context of criminal investigations. However, its clause b does indicate that any legally constituted government department that has interfaces with the public has rights over personal, transactional data.

> *(b) the processing of personal data by any court or tribunal or any other body in India which is entrusted by law with the performance of any judicial or quasi-judicial or regulatory or supervisory function, where such processing is necessary for the performance of such function**

This does give the GoI extraordinary powers to put into practice the principle of data exceptionalism. The DPDPA, 2023, while mandating significant data fiduciaries such as Google and other platforms to obtain user consent, waives such requirements for plain data fiduciaries including start-ups while giving the GoI final oversight over personal data (Singh:2023). Madan et al. (2023) in a legal analysis of the DPDPB have commented on the range of exemptions given to the GoI and the expansion of its control over personal data in India. "...sub-section (2) (in the section on Exemptions) affords Central Government sweeping exemptions from the application of provisions of DPDPB, while processing personal data. This ensures far-reaching and arbitrary powers given to the Central Government to interfere, monitor, retain and collect data, and effectively breach or invade privacy of individuals, in stark breach of their right to privacy and security".

These examples suggest that the gig economy in India will be shaped by policies that are opaque and ambivalent and in which the security of personal data will be at stake. The monetisation of personal data by the GoI for which consent is not taken and the ethics-free uses of personal data by start-ups are directly antithetical to the principles related to consent that have been included in the DPDPB. It is also clear that the start-up sector in India has played its part in creating the focus on 'significant data fiduciaries' and their responsibilities in the DPDPB at the expense of their own responsibilities with respect to the management of personal data. In fact, a number of start-ups including Paytm, Bharat Matrimony, Sharechat and others have written a dissenting note to the Committee on Digital Competition Law that was established by the GoI in February 2023 specifically to look into the need for ex-ante regulations for digital markets in the proposed Digital Competitions Bill in response to a submission made by the trade body, the Internet and Mobile Association of India (IAMAI), to ensure that these regulations apply only to Big Tech 'gate-keepers' referred to as 'systematically important digital intermediaries' (See Mathi:2023). The IAMAI, in their submission, had reiterated that they were not in favour of any new ex-ante regulations, a position that was contested by local platforms. "They are of the view that the extant rules and regulations sufficiently address competition concerns arising from the digital sector, while keeping the digital industry on a level playing field with other industries. The Competition Commission of India (CCI) has been promptly looking into various digital competition issues and has passed orders imposing penalties and requiring changes in the conduct of digital markets. Furthermore, the recent Competition (Amendment) Act, 2023 bolsters the existing regulatory framework for addressing competition issues in India" (IAMAI:2023). Irrespective of the need or not for ex-ante regulations, it is quite extraordinary that trade bodies such as the IAMAI simply do not want to consider the lessons from the Hindenburg expose of the Adani Group and the unravelling of Byju's in the matter of corporate governance.

Anti-Trust and the Competitions Commission of India

At any given time, the Competitions Commission of India is involved in anti-trust investigations against Big Tech in particular Amazon, Apple, Facebook (Meta), Google and local platform leaders such as Flipkart, Zomato and Swiggy among others. The Parliamentary Standing Committee on Finance did present a report entitled 'Anti-Competitive Practices by Big Tech Companies' to both houses of Parliament on 22 December 2022 (Economic Times:2023). This 84-page report discusses a number of issues including anti-steering provisions, platform neutrality/self-preferencing, bundling and tying, data usage, mergers and acquisitions, pricing/deep discounting, exclusive tie-ups, search and ranking preference, restricting third-party applications, advertising policies and ex-ante restraint. The report highlights the difference between traditional and digital markets and the latter's 'learning and network effects' that tend to result in monopolies both in core and adjacent markets resulting in winner-take-all consequences. On page 5, under the section on Anti-Steering provisions, the report highlights the monopoly that Google has in relation to App stores, especially Google Play and the "mandatory use of Play's payment system for paid apps & in-app purchases" and how it "restricts the choice available to the app developers to select a payment processing system of their choice' with Google charging a commission for 30 per cent for all app purchases". It also notes that Google Play is the "dominant source of downloading apps in the Android system (90 percent of the download)". The Committee also recommended that a specialised unit on digital markets be established within the CCI (39) (Anti-Competitive Practices by Big Tech Companies:2022). In October 2022, the CCI had fined Google Rs. 1337.76 crores for its abuse of its power in its Android market practices and a further Rs. 936.44 crores for abusing its dominant position related to Google Play Store billing practices (Aryan:2023). A year earlier in 2021 the CCI had begun an investigation on WhatsApp's notification to its users that it would share user data with its parent company Facebook, the first time that the CCI has dealt with platforms and privacy-related matters (Singh & Kumar:2021). However, the CCI's track record on anti-competitive practices has not been perfect. A good example is their ruling on the case brought by Bharti Airtel against Reliance Jio in 2016 for predatory pricing and for penetrating the market using unfair practices. As per The Competitions Act, 2002 "(b) "predatory price" means the sale of goods or provision of services, at a price which is below the cost, as may be determined by regulations, of production of the goods or provision of services, with a view to reduce competition or eliminate the competitors" (7). In this particular case, the CCI ruled that since Reliance Jio's share of the market was around 7 per cent as opposed to Bharti Airtel's market share of 23 per cent, neither zero pricing, free voice calls for life, free of cost or below cost offers that were part of the 'Jio Welcome Offer' for which data, voice, video and other applications were given free to subscribers for four months nor their control over a large portion of the 4G spectrum or the fact that they were being bankrolled by the parent company Reliance Industries were reasons to pull them up for being anti-competitive.

> The Commission notes that providing free services cannot by itself raise competition concerns unless the same is offered by a dominant enterprise and shown to be tainted with an anti-competitive objective of excluding competition/competitors, which does not seem to be the case in the instant matter as the relevant market is characterised by the presence of entrenched players with sustained business presence and financial strength. In a competitive market scenario, where there are already big players operating in the market, it would not be anticompetitive for an entrant to incentivise customers towards its own services by giving attractive offers and schemes. Such short-term business strategy of an entrant to penetrate the market and establish its identity cannot be considered to be anti-competitive in nature and as such cannot be a subject matter of investigation under the Act.
>
> (CCI, Case 3, 2017, 15–16)

Seven years after this ruling in August 2023, the three dominant players – Jio, Airtel and Vodafone between them accounted for 91 per cent of subscribers with Jio's total subscriber base at 438.6 (38.35 per cent) and Airtel's at 373.7 (32.7 per cent) (ET Telecom:2023)! By 2019, Airtel had incurred losses of Rs. 2,866 crores while Vodafone Idea had lost Rs 4,874 crores (Kore & Yadav:2020), a reality that suggests that the issue was predation rather than just plain competition. The CCI's ruling in this particular case does suggest that they are faced with major challenges in trying to create a level playing field by providing clear limits to entry barriers given the economic power of both transnational and local firms and platforms – referred to as Systematically Important Digital Intermediaries in the report on anti-competitive practices. This ruling also suggests that the CCI is unwilling to deal with predatory pricing especially when companies such as Reliance have established their dominance by riding on the coat-tails of Made in India, data localisation and data sovereignty. Furthermore, the CCI simply has to reckon with the fact that Reliance Jio belongs to the largest conglomerate in India, Reliance Industries, a company that has multifaceted business interests across more productive sectors in India from oil and gas to retail and the media.

The CCI's stance is markedly different from the Federal Trade Commission in the USA that under the present commissioner Lina Khan (2017:713) it has attempted to understand the complex means by which anti-competitive behaviour is currently manifested in and through dominant platforms in the USA. Khan has in particular explored the anti-competitive behaviour of Amazon that very like Reliance is not just involved in its core business, the latter being involved in petrochemicals and the former in e-commerce but that

> In addition to being a retailer,... is a marketing platform, a delivery and logistics network, payment service, a credit lender, an auction house, a major book publisher, a producer of television and films, a fashion designer, a hardware manufacturer, and a leading provider of cloud service space and computing power.

As Khan has observed, Amazon has evaded regulatory scrutiny because of both its public narrative and the reality of reducing costs for consumers. Anti-competitive behaviour in platform markets cannot be gauged by price and output alone but by investigating the structuring role that it plays in creating market dynamics, how anti-competitive conflicts of interests are manifested across its businesses, how its market dominance is cross-leveraged across sectors and how the market itself contributes to maintain the status quo based on the primacy of network effects in data markets (717). Khan argues that at the core of anti-competition policy should be the presumption of predation and restrictions to vertical integration. She goes one step further – if indeed these data markets are favourable to monopolies or oligopolies, then these firms should be treated as public utilities (803). In other words, Khan advocates for a structural separation because this would "eliminate the incentives that would make that conduct possible or likely in the first place" (Khan, 2019:980).

In contrast to the strident measures advocated by Lina Khan, both the case of Byju's and Adani does suggest that the GoI's approach is dictated by the priority of growth, Made in India and the absolute imperative to transform India into a multi-trillion dollar economy at the expense of governance and regulation. While the Company Law Committee established by the Ministry of Corporate Affairs, 2019 does plan to advocate for stronger regulation of start-ups in the light of scandals such as that of Byju's, there is as yet, very little information available on the extent of this regulation. Start-ups in India have traditionally been given extraordinary incentives with minimum standards of compliance. So, for example, start-ups are required to self-certify their compliance with six labour and three environmental legislations and are exempted for three years from complying with other labour-related legislations as per the Companies Act, 2013:

> **Labour Laws**: • Other Constructions Workers' (Regulation of Employment & Conditions of Service) Act, 1996 • The Inter-State Migrant Workmen (Regulation of Employment & Conditions of Service) Act, 1979 • The Payment of Gratuity Act, 1972 • The Contract Labour (Regulation and Abolition) Act, 1970 • The Employees' Provident Funds and Miscellaneous Provisions Act, 1952 • The Employees' State Insurance Act, 1948 **Environment Laws**: • The Water (Prevention & Control of Pollution) Act, 1974 • The Water (Prevention & Control of Pollution) Cess (Amendment) Act, 2003 • The Air (Prevention & Control of Pollution) Act, 1981. Additionally, start-ups are only required to provide minimum financial statements, enjoy various tax benefits including exemptions on profits and gains, from angel tax, on capital gains from investment in specific funds and on residential property.
>
> (See Thinking Legal:n.d.)

While the gig economy is thriving in India despite the lack of governance and some evidence of 'flipping', successful initiatives relocating to countries where it is easier to operate from, it remains an enclave economy contributing in a major way to India's GDP while employing a tiny percentage of people in India's labour market. There is a sense in which start-ups and venture capitals are making a mark in every productive sector in the Indian economy including in agriculture where there are any number of start-ups involved in 'precision agriculture'. There has been a growth in the so-called UNICORNs – start-ups that have transformed into billion-dollar companies, numbering 110 in 2023, collectively worth $347 billion that India Inc. is proud of (Team Inc42:2023). While the statistics on the wealth of UNICORNS have become a story of an ascendent economic power, the statistics on the less-salubrious aspects of realities in India such as poverty have become highly politicised. It varies greatly precisely because of the different yardsticks used to understand poverty and the present government's penchant for embracing numbers in the lower end of the poverty scale. With neither the previous government nor the present supporting the National Consumption Expenditure Surveys conducted by the National Sample Survey Organisation (the NSSO's five-year surveys have been discontinued), the figures in the 2011–12 survey is 29.5 per cent or 363 million. There are 2022 accounts that estimate poverty at 2.5 per cent although there are others that indicate that it has risen to 26.9 per cent or 372.8 million (Iqbal:2023). While a flourishing gig economy and investments in various levels of its eco-system are vital to the country's economic future, there are other stories of labour and gig work, the informal economy and poverty that simply are not seen to be newsworthy because such stories can go against the grain of a resurgent Indian economy, a cashless society in which start-up millionaires and the connected masses live in a frictionless, national community. Arguably, the gig economy is not just about Swiggy and Uber, their clients and workers but also those who know about how to exploit the grey areas in digital transactions. Jamtara in Jharkhand and the Mewat region covering Haryana, Rajasthan and Uttar Pradesh have become the epi-centres of the cyberscam industry focussed largely on scamming locally in India while Kolkatta has a 'phishing' industry that operates from call centres (Free Press Journal:2023). Some of these scammers are migrant workers who were displaced by demonetisation and Covid and have now found an easy way to make money. Perhaps, there is a lesson here for a government that did not think through the consequences of its hasty actions. Noida is home to a thriving scamming industry that specifically focuses on the vulnerable elderly in the USA by using stolen Social Security Numbers that are available on the dark web (Mint:2023). Those involved in the scams in Noida include educated locals who are attracted to the prospect of making a generous income. Since making money is the key objective in the gig economy, there are more than ways to make money. In other words, the story of digital India and the start-up State is not just about the 'official' version but also about the many 'unofficial' *Jugaad* varieties of people using the technological architectures available and devices such as smartphones to exploit people's lack of cybersecurity literacy. Who benefits from all this growth and how is an important question to ask as we deal with the complex, sprawling and largely unregulated multifaceted gig economy in India.

Bibliography

Adil, M. H. & Hatekar, N. R. (2020), Demonetisation, Banking and Trust in 'Bricks' or 'Clicks' (181–198), *South Asia Research*, 40 (2).

Anti-Competitive Practices by Big Tech Companies (2022, 1–84), Standing Committee on Finance (2022–2023), Seventeenth Lok Sabha, Ministry of Corporate Affairs, Fifty Third Report, Lok Sabha Secretariat, New Delhi. Available at: https://eparlib.nic.in/bitstream/123456789/1464505/1/17_Finance_53.pdf

Aryan, A. (2023), Law in the Works to Curb Big Tech's Digital Dominance after CCI Ruling, *The Economic Times*, April 12. Available at: https://economictimes.indiatimes.com/tech/technology/law-in-the-works-to-curb-big-techs-digital-dominance-after-cci-ruling/articleshow/99414619.cms?from=mdr

Chakraborty, S. (2023), Indian Corporate Governance Comes Under Fire as Byjus Stumbles, *NikkeiAsia*, July 3. Available at: https://asia.nikkei.com/Spotlight/Market-Spotlight/Indian-corporate-governance-comes-under-fire-as-Byju-s-stumbles

Competition Commission Conducting Enquiries against Big Tech Companies: Govt. (2023), *Retail.com: Economic Times*, March 29. Available at: https://retail.

economictimes.indiatimes.com/news/e-commerce/e-tailing/competition-commission-conducting-inquiries-against-big-tech-companies-govt/99075841#:~:text=2%20min%20read-,Competition%20Commission%20conducting%20inquiries%20against%20big%20tech%20companies%3A%20Govt,for%20alleged%20anti%2Dcompetitive%20practices

Competition Commission of India Case No. 3 of 2017 (2017), Bharti Airtel Ltd vs. reliance Industries Ltd/reliance Jio Infocomm Ltd. (1–17), New Delhi. Available at: https://www.cci.gov.in/antitrust/orders/details/335/0

https://hindenburgresearch.com/adani/

IAMAI members flag concerns regarding ex-ante regulations (2023), IAMAI, May 16. Availableat:https://www.medianama.com/wp-content/uploads/2023/06/IAMAI-PR-on-Digital-Competition-Law.pdf

IANS, From sextortion to OLX scams, Mewat leaves Jamtara behind in cyber crimes (2023), *The Free Press Journal*, February 19. Available at: https://www.freepressjournal.in/india/from-sextortion-to-olx-scams-mewat-leaves-jamtara-behind-in-cyber-crimes

India's Unicorn Club: Here's the Comprehensive List of 100+ Unicorns in India (2023), *Inc42*, August 14. Available at: https://inc42.com/features/indias-unicorn-club-the-comprehensive-list-of-unicorns-in-india/

Iqbal, N. (2023) How Many People Live below the Poverty Line in India? It Could Be 34 Million or 373 Million, *Scroll.in*, May 5. Available at: https://scroll.in/article/1048475/how-many-people-live-below-the-poverty-line-in-india-it-could-be-34-million-or-373-million

Jain, A. & Jain, S. (2023), Deciphering Corporate Misgovernance at Indian Startups, *Deccan Herald*, June 26. Available at: https://www.deccanherald.com/business/deciphering-corporate-misgovernance-at-indian-startups-1231165.html

Jain, S. & Gabor, D. (2020), The Rise of Digital Financialisation: The Case of India (813–828), *New Political Economy*, 25(5).

Karwowski, E. (2019), Towards (De-)financialisation: The Role of the State (1001–1027), *Cambridge Journal of Economics*, 43.

Khan, L. (2017) Amazon's Anti-Trust Paradox (710–805), *The Yale Law Review*, 126(3).

Khan, L. (2019), The Separation of Platforms and Commerce (973–1098), *Colombia Law Review*, 119(4).

Kore, S. & Yadav, J. (2020), Attempt to Monopolisation and Digital Markets: Enforcement Gap (103–122), *Competition Commission of India Journal on Competition Law and Policy*, 1.

Kumar, A. (2023) Why Has the Adani-Hindenburg Issue Become a Matter of National Concern, *The Wire*, May 26. Available at: https://thewire.in/business/why-has-the-adani-hindenburg-issue-become-a-matter-of-national-concern

Madan, N., Joseph, V., Mendiratta, U., Soni, J., Rai, S., Aneja, R. & Karanth, S. (2023), The Digital Personal Data Protection Bill, 2022 – An Analysis, Lexology, April 12. Availableat:https://www.lexology.com/library/detail.aspx?g=22006942-bb22-4be8-98c4-f4b5ef2186b4

Mathi, S. (2023), Why Some Start-Ups Are Disagreeing with IAMAI's Stance on Digital Competition Bill and Ex-Ante Regulations, *Medianama*, June 21. Available at:https://www.medianama.com/2023/06/223-startups-dissent-note-iamai-stance-digital-competition-bill/

Nair, V. (2019), Governing India in Cybertime: Biometric IDs, Start-Ups and the Temporalised State (519–536), *South Asia: Journal of South Asian Studies*, 42(3).

Noida Call Centres Swindles Thousands of Americans; 84 Arrested, Including 38 Women (2023), *Mint*, August 28. Available at: https://www.livemint.com/news/india/noida-call-centre-swindles-thousands-of-americans-84-arrested-including-38-women-11693201614285.html

Pai, T.V.M. & Baid, Y. (2021), India, a Start-Up Nation, *India Global Business*, August 6. Available at: https://www.indiaglobalbusiness.com/industry/startups/india-a-start-up-nation

Rault, Y.-M., Mathew, S. (2019), An Imbalanced Ecosystem: Start-Ups in India (45–50), *Economic & Political Weekly*, LIV(45).

Regulatory framework for start-ups in India (n.d.), *Thinking Legal*. Available at: http://thinkinglegal.in/demo/sites/default/files/Regulatory%20Framework%20for%20Startups%20in%20India.pdf

Reliance Jio Outpaces Bharti Airtel, Adds Most Wireless Users in June (2023), ET Telecom.com, Economic Times, August 24. Available at: https://telecom.economictimes.indiatimes.com/news/industry/reliance-jio-outpaces-bharti-airtel-adds-most-wireless-users-in-june/103029674

Sebastian, M. (2023), Byju's: The Unravelling of India's Most Valued Start-Up, *BBC*, July 10. Available at: https://www.bbc.com/news/world-asia-india-66126095

Singh, A. P. & Kumar, H. (2021), Anti-trust Regulators vs. Big Tech: The Battle Reaches India, *Oxford Business Law Blogs*, July 22. Available at: https://blogs.law.ox.ac.uk/business-law-blog/blog/2021/07/antitrust-regulators-v-big-tech-battle-reaches-india

Singh, J. (2023),India pushes ahead with data privacy bill despite pushback from critics, *TechCrunch*, August 7. Available at: https://techcrunch.com/2023/08/07/india-digital-data-privacy-bill/

Subramaniam, N. (2023), National Start-Up Day: A Day for New India, *Inc42*, January 15. Available at: https://inc42.com/features/national-startup-day-a-day-for-new-india/

Sureban, H. (2023), Corporate Governance: The Missing Link in the Indian Start-Up System, July 16, *The Hindu Business Line*. Available at: https://www.thehindubusinessline.com/specials/emerging-entrepreneurs/the-missing-link-in-the-indian-start-up-ecosystem/article67086799.ece

The Competitions Act, 2002 (1–65). Available at: https://www.cci.gov.in/images/legalframeworkact/en/the-competition-act-20021652103427.pdf

The Digital Personal Data Protection Act, 2023, Ministry of Law & Justice, *The Gazette of India*, August 11. Available at: https://www.meity.gov.in/writereaddata/files/Digital%20Personal%20Data%20Protection%20Act%202023.pdf

3 Venture Capitalism, Informality and the Gig Economy

A Brief History of the Gig Economy

While it is difficult to precisely date the advent of the platform-work economy in India, the growth of Business Process Outsourcing in India that paralleled India becoming a key source for global software exports two decades ago offered entry-level workers with little more than high school education an opportunity to be involved in a variety of backend work, such as medical transcription, as data workers for a variety of multinational companies including banks and credit card companies, travel and transportation and logistics. The flexibility of such work and salaries that were much better than what was offered in other types of employment in the unorganised sector also led to the entry of women into this type of work. This work continues to be in demand today although the specific character of online work has changed and includes work such as 'crowdsourced' editorial services, web development and translation among other types of both high and low-end piecemeal work and content moderation for all the major search and sociality platforms (See D'Cruz and Noronha:2023). The Covid pandemic that necessitated multiple shutdowns provided the perfect opportunity for the scaling up of both home-based work and home-delivery and the creation of any number of platforms involved in the servicing of populations who were restricted from movement and who were under curfew regulations. To the enormous numbers of people who became unemployed due to the closure of both urban and rural employment generators during the pandemic, platform work became an option because of the flexibility that it offered.

Typically, the word 'platform' in India is used to describe digital infrastructures, apps, e-portals, social media sites and technologies that enable transactional flows. Mukherjee (2019:176–77) in an article on the disruptive control of the mobile market launched by Jio describes platforms in India as follows

> In India, platform has often been used to describe both the plethora of apps targeted toward the rapidly growing smartphone users and the e-portals that the Indian government launches as part of its e-governance initiatives. What unites these apps and web/mobile portals together is

DOI: 10.4324/9781003491705-4

their identification with the Web 2.0 services, and "platforms" have thus become another name for such Web 2.0 enabled/supported apps and portals.

This rather generous and inclusive interpretation of platforms does point to the fact that an app is nothing without a platform and vice versa although the overlaps and blurrings do not allow for any analytical precision. The platform ecosystem in other words consists of a technological architecture in an intermediary role that enables transactions and flows. It enables technologies that connect with the platform used by consumers (mobile phones) and producers as is the case with Amazon and apps that facilitate a direct connection with consumers without the need for an intermediary, for example, FinTech apps that connect to a client and precision agriculture-linked apps that connect with a farmer's mobile phone. There are probably many other permutations in this era of start-ups and unicorns although the attrition rate is high following consolidation in specific sectors such as food and grocery delivery (Poovanna:2022). Nick Srnicek (2017:48) in his concise text on platform capitalism describes the core function of platforms as the business of extracting, controlling and monetising data. 'Platforms…are a new type of firm; they are characterised by providing the infrastructure to intermediate between different user groups, by displaying monopoly tendencies driven by network effects, by employing cross-subsidisation to draw in different user groups, and by having a designed core architecture that governs the interaction possibilities'. Of course, behind platforms are the increasingly vast footprint of cloud and data centres that store transactional data – another part of the gig economy jigsaw that is simply foundational. In this chapter and volume, the focus will be on platforms that are specifically related to the digital gig economy, their political economy and the ecosystem.

The GoI has played an important role in contributing to the ecology of platforms and start-ups by establishing digital public goods such as UPI that facilitate nationwide business-to-consumer, business-to-business and government-to-consumer financial transactions, along with initiatives such as Start-Up India's 19-point action plan that includes access to seed funding and a three-year tax exemption (See #startupindia:n.d.). The Indian state is playing an important role in nurturing a form of entrepreneurial capitalism and is involved in the process of 'governing through financial markets' (See Santos:2022), a state-led financialisation in which financial institutions, markets and financial elites are valued as significant contributors to the growth of the platform economy in India. Coolman (2021:233) describes these elites as 'monetary technocrats' who are entangled with the public sector through their investments and partnerships and who exert infrastructural power given their involvement in policymaking. 'These entanglements become two-way streets: state actors send their capital along these streets to achieve policy goals, and financial actors may use the streets to make demands, positioning themselves as gatekeepers at essential junctions'. In other words, these enmeshings are mutually beneficial and like technocrats, monetary technocrats are as well, well-regarded by the GoI. The GoI, for example, was involved in establishing the Technology Development and Information Company of India Ltd in 1988, India's largest and oldest venture capital (VC) funds that was a joint venture between the ICICI and the Unit Trust of India (UTI). Today, there are three types of VCs that are promoted by the Central government, state governments and private funds. The Tamilnadu government, for example, has launched the Tamilnadu Emerging Sector Seed Fund specifically to help start-ups and most states in India have. Banks and institutional lenders as well have contributed to this ecology.

Venture Capital in the Gig Economy

> Venture financing is a continuous process of simultaneously funding and exiting, by rolling over funds from one entity to another. As these firms are privately held, funding and shareholder agreements are opaque. Venture financing is a stacked deck, where different venture funds come in at successive stages to acquire a stake in the firm while earlier funds may either continue or cash out of the deal. Financing involves different combinations of equity and debt. Typically, the share of venture capital in a high-value startup would be around 70% to 80%, with the founders, employee stock ownership plans (ESOPs), and other shareholders accounting for the rest. The realisation of returns is through a process euphemistically described as an exit. Between 2015 and 2020, the top seven global VCFs in India raised approximately US$9.5 billion, deployed US$7.3 billion in several venture deals, and realised an exit value of US$12.6 billion. This amounts to a total return of 72% or a CAGR of more than 18% on investment over an average holding period of four years.
>
> (Jayaram:2022)

The role played by VCs and venture capitalists have been critical to the growth of start-ups specifically within the digital gig economy. Venture capitalists who have been critical to the success of Silicon Valley are typically investors who are willing to invest in an innovation in return for a share in the equity of a start-up. They exist because of the structure of capital markets, and government rules and regulations that established financial institutions such as banks in investing in endeavours that are potentially risky. If in the USA, a company could go public only if they had sales of $15 million and assets of $10 million in India, the Securities and Exchange Board of India stipulatesthat a company can make an Initial Public Offering (IPO) only if they had a pre-tax profit across three years of US$1.8 million, tangible assets worth US$363,000 and a net worth of US$122,222 (=1 Crore) (See SEBI: Issues by Indian Companies in India).

As Zider (1998) describes in an article in the Harvard Business Review, 'Venture capital fills the void between sources of funds for innovation (chiefly corporations, government bodies, and the entrepreneur's friends and family) and traditional, lower-cost sources of capital available to ongoing concerns. Filling that void successfully requires the venture capital industry to provide a sufficient return on capital to attract private equity funds, attractive returns for its own participants, and sufficient upside potential to entrepreneurs to attract high-quality ideas that will generate high returns. Put simply, the challenge is to earn a consistently superior return on investments in inherently risky business ventures'. Today, the role of venture capitalists is critical to the success of platforms in India. There are a range of VCs investing in India and this includes Global VCs, Domestic VCs, direct investment from Sovereign Funds and large corporates such as Reliance, Microsoft, Amazon Inc. and Alphabet Inc. While there are specialised VCs who invest in particular sectors such as fintech, Web 3.0 and Consumer tech, there are many that have a diverse investment portfolio across a range of start-ups. A list of the 58 most active venture capitalists in India and their investment priorities quite categorically include start-ups, predominantly in different parts of the tech sector in outsourcing, mobile, internet, cloud-enabled services, data infrastructure, big data analytics, data security, telecom equipment retail, financial services and more recently in AI, Blockchain, Robotics and the Internet of Things (See Inc42:n.d.). While average deals were between 12 and 25 million, a handful of companies including Swiggy were able to raise $500 mn in a single round of investments. Despite a slow-down in VC investments in India in the immediate post-Covid years caused by the repercussions of the war in Ukraine, rise in interest rates, perceived lack of returns on investments and low-risk attitudes, VC investments in India in 2022 in 1129 firms were worth $20.8 billion (Mehra:2022). It is nevertheless worth pointing out that in 2021 VC investment was in the area of US$38.5 bn and the valuation of the 50,000+ start-ups in India is $400 bn (Sable:2022). However, this valuation is now considered as an overvaluation and in 2023 there has been a sharp decline in exogenous VC investments in India with $2 bn raised in the first quarter which is 75 per cent less than what it was in the previous year. The most problematic issue has been overvaluation – with the Hindenburg Report on the Adani Group earlier in 2023 making this issue globally salient. In 2023, the investment group Blackrock cut the valuation of the Indian ed-tech company and India's most valued start-up Byju's by half, US$22 bn to US$11.5 bn, while Swiggy's valuation was similarly downgraded by Invesco from $10.7 bn to $5.5bn, a 48.6 per cent decrease (See Singh:2023b; Singh:2023c). Venture capitalists are typically involved in the short term (often 6 years) and their exit is a measure of the success of this type of investment (IPO, strategic sale, secondary sale and buyback), although exits can also be the result of a catastrophic failure (liquidation) of a given start-up. Dominic & Gopalswamy (2019:148) have observed that between 2000 and 2017 out of 481 exits, the bulk (280) were in the IT and ITES industries, followed by non-financial services (73) and banking and financial services industries (43) with the least in healthcare, retail and life sciences industries. It is unsurprising that the IT and ITES sectors have traditionally attracted VCs since it is an established contributor to both the Indian and global economy and is characterised by 'shorter entrepreneurial cycles, high innovation quotient, and lower investment requirements' (Dugar & Basant, 2021:283). Venture capitalists are typically involved in hedging risk against high returns in cycles that include financing, valuation and exit.

From the inception of the Start-up India programme in 2016 to 2023, there have been close to 57 start-up-related regulations and notifications to enhance ease of business, tax breaks and reduce the burden of compliance (Draft Compendium of StartUp Specific Initiatives). There are at least 16 major government schemes to help start-ups in India including the Pradhan Mantri Mudra Yojna, the Atal Innovation Mission, the Venture Capital Assistance Scheme and the Standup India scheme among others. While the services sector's contributions to India's GDP have increased over the years, the bulk of workers are in agriculture. This is the sector that is continuing to go through a severe crisis and the distress of agricultural workers that has been graphically reflected in farm suicides in different parts of the country is a story that is barely being told in India's legacy media. Investigative reporter P Sainath's People's Archive of Rural India carries stories of this other India that has experienced a relentless decline in living standards. The government's captivation of entrepreneurs and start-ups stands in stark contrast to its investments in a sector that has steadily fallen over the years. These include a slash in subsidies to agricultural inputs such as credit, pesticides and fertilisers, the removal of restrictions to agricultural imports, increased costs of banking and credit to agricultural workers and cut back on development expenditure (Athreya:2021) that culminated in the promulgation of three farm laws that would have led to increased corporatisation of the production, distribution and pricing of agricultural products. These bills were withdrawn in 2022 after a year-long strike by farmers from Punjab, India's major wheat- and grain-growing state. Such disinvestments in a sector stand in marked contrast to the support given to digital growth and productivity – and yet this support is for the entrepreneurs, not for the gig workers who are key to growth in the platform economy.

Investments in fintech have been particularly marked. In the context of a weak regulatory environment, transactional data collected from customers have been used to create credit risk analysis for customers and a market segmentation that ironically also includes gig workers. However, fintech's disruptive potential is particularly an issue in the context of older industries such as the banking sector where cryptocurrencies and new forms of financial intermediation have forced this older legacy system to adapt to a context in which segmented customers are being serviced by an extensive array of financial services. Bank's traditional dominance in 'payments' is under threat from fintech. Langley and Leyshon (2021:381) in an article on the political economy of fintech point to the impact of this sector on the so-called 'unbanked' people who include gig workers. The GoI's key objective with respect to India Stack is to achieve digital financial inclusivity although its consequences could include the disintermediation of traditional, informal 'monetary and financial relations'. Sudeep Jain and Daniela Gabor (2020) have argued that both demonetisation and Direct Benefits Transfer (DBT) are mechanisms used by the GoI to increase the demand for digitally mediated financial services at the expense of cash transactions. This has impacted the relationship between the formal and informal economies that traditionally were based on the exchange of cash. So, the informal economy is being forced to become formal although one can argue that the tenor and cultural register of informality are much deeper than a change to a payments and remittances regime. The questions that they pose at the end of the article on the larger implications of this shift towards digital financialisation are important for us to consider in the context of a weak regulatory regime and economic vulnerabilities that are specifically experienced by the millions of people involved in the informal economy. '(1) What are the implications for the nature of money, monetary policy and financial stability of a system where banks are not the primary providers of payments services and which is not regulated by the central bank? (2) What role does the state envision for itself in the digital age, not just in the financial sector but in all realms, particularly in what concerns a rethinking of developmental states in the digital age? (3) What are the social, cultural political forces at play which allow states and companies to get away with high levels of monitoring and coercion?' (824). These questions need to be asked precisely because the fintech landscape in India is also a space where a great many predatory fast-track lending companies operate. In July 2023, the App Store in India withdrew a number of apps including Pocket Kash, White Kash, Golden Kash and OK Rupee for their extortionate charges and dubious methods of loan recovery (Singh:2023a). However, this is a tiny sliver of the fast-loan apps in the Apple Store that number in the hundreds. A Reserve Bank of India investigation from 1 January 1 to 28 February 2020 found 600 predatory apps while Google Play enforced actions against 3,500 loan apps in 2023 (Rohit:2023). Fast-track lending companies are part of an ecosystem that includes loan recovery firms such as Callflex Corporation and Majesty Legal Services and organisations involved in assessing creditworthiness such as CreditVidya. CreditVidya's Software Development Kit (SDK) is embedded in the loan company's app and as collateral, it controls and monitors all transactions on the phone including SMS texts, contacts, location and all installed apps (See CreditVidya:n.d.). A 2023 report in the BBC highlights the fact that over 60 people took their own lives after being harassed by loan app companies to repay loans (Agarwal, Sonr & Hegarty:2023).

While there literally are hundreds of firms involved in fintech India at the moment, it will be interesting to see whether Big Tech will be able to consolidate its control over fintech as they have over other sectors such as Cloud and data centres in India. In other words, fintech consolidations can happen in India just as they have in other parts of the world – 'rather than enhance competition in existing retail money and financial markets, platform reintermediation seeks to produce new market structures that will secure new oligopolistic and monopolistic positions' (385).

Informality and the Gig Economy in India

While the gig economy linked to a variety of digital mediations of services in India is lauded as a new opportunity for employment by the State and Big Tech, it is important that we assess its characteristics in the light of the reality of employment in India in the post-Independent era. It is a fact that gig work or as what economists would describe as work in the informal economy accounts for more than 85 per cent of workers in India. In other words, hardly 15 per cent of the workforce in India are in formal employment whose conditions are guaranteed by legal provisions and whose monthly wages are backed up by gratuity, provident fund and trade unions. The informal sector accounts for the bulk of those involved in agricultural work, construction, mining, manufacturing of everyday essential food and non-food items, servicing of cities (domestic help, security staff, brokers and fixers, those involved in the literally thousands of jobs from ironing services to laundry and gardening). The informal sector, taken in its entirety, is in this sense integrated into and critical to the workings of the formal economy. Informalisation of the workforce and the casualisation of work are also a reality in the formal economy – in both the public sector, for example, contractual work in the Railways in India, and in the corporate sector.

Notes on the Precariat

Guy Standing (2011) had written an influential treatise on what he described as the *Precariat: The New Dangerous Class* based on his recognition of the growing army of the underclass and their presence and work across many sectors of the service economy in the West. The precariat as a descriptor has especially been used to describe workers in the digital gig economy and the conditions of their employment that are circumscribed by algorithmic management and dispensability. While Standing's contribution alerted observers and policymakers to the growing emergence of a 'class in waiting' involved in a distinct employment stream with its attendant opportunities and challenges, Ronaldo Munck (2013:752) in an article published in the *Third World Quarterly* queried the originality of the term and its applicability 'What is most noticeable in the broader literature around precarity and the precariat is that it is almost totally Northern-centric in its theoretical frames and empirical reference points. There is a totally Northern sensibility at play here, it seems. In Standing's case it is really just Britain that is the model of economic and political development which he has in mind. There is hardly a reference any part of the world outside the North Atlantic. It is simply assumed as the centre and the norm which will apply everywhere. There is little cognisance the type of work described by the term 'precarity' has always been the norm the global South'. Munck's critique is an important one because it forces us to recognise the fact that the condition of precarity has always been and continues to envelop the majority of working lives and livelihoods in the so-called least developing and developing worlds – a reality that will remain irrespective of smartphone ownership, e-government and increasingly transactional lives lived under the promises of the Digital India sublime.

The Informal Economy in India

While there have been a number of academics who have explored the informal economy in India (Basile:2013, Breman:1996, Barnes: 2015, Mitra, A. (2014), Bhattacharya and Kesar:2020, Marjit & Kar:2011, among others), Barbara Harriss-White's (2017, 2020, 2019) interventions and interpretations based on her work in Tamilnadu provides both a macro perspective on informality in India and insights that can be applied to an understanding of the digital gig economy in India. In Harriss-White's assessment (2017), the informal economy in India is not an aberration but a critical contributor to the Indian economy – 60 per cent of the GDP, 40 per cent of manufactured exports are produced by 45 million small firms, 90 per cent of work is unregistered and within the state and private sectors and 40–80 per cent of jobs are sub-contracted (1728). In other words, the State while publicly celebrating the formal economy has a complex relationship with a sector that typically does not come under the formal embrace of the regulatory and taxation regimes but with which it has to negotiate simply because the vast majority of voters belong to this sector as agricultural workers and those involved in a variety of trades across all cities in India, irrespective of whether these are considered Tier 1 or not. To Harriss-White, the informal economy is not in any sense a failure 'but a result of deliberate neglect' (1735) by a State that recognises the values of the skills of a machinist and small traders to economic growth (1736). Jan Breman's (1996:23) work on the informal economy in the districts of Valsad, Surat and Dang in South Gujarat highlights a move away from informal labour from agriculture to non-agricultural labour although she notes that this change merely led to a great incidence of migratory labour '....expansion of the non-agrarian economy has not brought a commensurate increase in informal sector labour in towns and cities, while informal sector employment in the countryside has not formalized, even when there was good reason for it. Mobilization of casual labour, hired and fired according to the needs of the moment, and transported for the duration of the job to destinations far distant from the home village, is characteristic of the capitalist regime presently dominating in South Asia'.

In her fieldwork in Arni, Tamilnadu, Harriss-White in her assessment of innovation in the informal economy, highlights the presence of digital production and digital labour that contributes to both the formal and informal economies. 'A back-alley "computer centre" combines novel forms of collective ownership and part-time management; instalment payment systems; process innovation (3-D software); capacity-building for product innovation (computer-aided design); capacity building in the English language for poorly educated rural clients and informal certification of competence'

(1743). When this computer centre is seen in relation to the literally thousands of such centres spread over the country offering both entry-level and high-end services, the informal economy certainly functions as a foot-soldier for the formal economy, democratising access to the digital, while practising the right to repair and *jugaad* innovations and adaptations that contribute to a levelling of access to externalities and connecting selectively to the transactional practices that are at the heart of the vision of Digital India.

While there are distinctive characteristics of the digital gig economy, it simply needs to be seen as a sector that is closely linked to the larger informal economy that pre-exists in India. In fact, the very same workers who work in the informal sector are often those who find work in the digital gig economy. The informal sector does fall under the ambit of the State that has traditionally treated this sector with benign neglect, although it can harass 'unlicensed' street vendors and destroy illegally constructed roadside habitations that have some legal electricity supplies in the context of road-widening projects while offering a safety net through MRNEGA and other employment projects, access to the PDS system and subsidised livelihood costs and arrangements. It has been argued that the demonetisation of 80 per cent of the notes in 2016 was an attempt by the State to short-circuit the predominance of cash transactions in the informal economy and force workers and small firms into adopting cashless behaviour. While there is evidence of the adoption of state-based financialisation efforts in the post-COVID period enabled by India Stack, it remains unclear as to whether the array of digital mission-level projects has led to less cash circulating in the informal sector (See Surie 2020). Given the State's relationship with this sector, the quality of its engagement with the digital gig economy and its workers is based on an older script although it is framed by the centrality of digital platforms to the Indian economy and concessions to their machine-enabled interpretations of labour, rights, work and compensation.

e-Shram

While the government has attempted to build a database of unorganised workers through its e-Shram (National Database of Unorganised Workers) portal, the complicated and complex requirement registration processes and limited language support (Hindi & English) have remained obstacles to the registration of gig workers. There are other more insidious issues that may have contributed to the lag in registration including the perception of constant government oversight over all government–citizen transactions and the centrality of the Aadhar interface and Aadhar intermediation for the unlocking of government support along with inordinately long delays in the implementation of welfare schemes for gig workers. The objectives of the e-Shram portal highlight the centralising nature of an initiative and its potential to control personal and private data:

- Creation of a centralized database of all unorganised workers (UWs) including construction workers, migrant workers, gig and platform workers, street vendors, domestic workers, agriculture workers, etc., to be seeded with Aadhaar.
- To improve the implementation efficiency of the social security services for the UWs.(ii) Integration of Social Security Schemes meant for UWs being administered by MoLE and subsequently those run by other ministries as well.
- Sharing of information in respect of registered UWs with various stakeholders such as Ministries/Departments/Boards/Agencies/Organisations of the central and state governments through APIs for delivery of various social security and welfare schemes being administered by them.
- Portability of the social security and welfare benefits to migrant and construction workers.
- Providing a comprehensive database to central and state governments for tackling any National Crises like COVID-19 in future (Objectives of e-Shram Portal).

The Lack of Gig Worker Protection

There are a number of media, market-based and public sector reports that indicate that platforms and the gig economy linked to platforms are increasing their share of contributions to the GDP in India in terms of employment and value. This is not entirely surprising given the representative salience of this sector and the increasing visibility of uniformed digital gig workers across all tiered cities in India. This public presence can be contrasted with the persistent invisibility of multifarious types of gig workers including landless labourers who have traditionally been involved in piecemeal work in agriculture, home help and hospitality among workers in very many 'unorganised' sectors. This latter army of workers who are largely in the 'unorganised' sectors make up close to 93 per cent of the 'employed' in India as wage workers, self-employed workers and home workers and who are incidentally not '..... covered by any of the Acts mentioned in Schedule-II of Act i.e. the Employee's Compensation Act, 1923 (3 of 1923), the Industrial Disputes Act, 1947 (14 of 1947), the Employees' State Insurance Act, 1948 (34 of 1948), the Employees Provident Funds and Miscellaneous Provision Act, 1952 (19 of 1952), the Maternity Benefit Act, 1961 (53 of 1961) and the Payment of Gratuity Act, 1972 (39 of 1972)' (GoI, Ministry of Labour & Employment). This vast army of traditional gig workers has played an absolutely critical role in the Indian economy in both India's colonial and pre-colonial past and its post-Independent present, although their representational claims are often ignored by the media in India that are fixated on skilled workers in the organised sector. Digital gig workers really are a sub-set of this much larger workforce and face the very same issues of 'legal' invisibility that traditional gig workers have faced. While there certainly have been in the recent past regional and national attempts at providing some form of security for these workers, their precarity has certainly contributed to the economic advantage of their employers – landlords, real estate companies involved in construction and platform-based entities such as Uber and Swiggy in India who have manipulated wages and/or distanced themselves from their employees by subjecting their piecemeal work to what platforms deem to be 'objective', but what really are opaque processes of algorithmic management. When looking at the history of the unorganised sector in India, there is evidence of social movement-based organising of landless labourers and other workers for better wages and working conditions. Gig workers in the platform economy have, until very recently, been unable to or proscribed from organising themselves. Their status as casual, gig workers and not employees has been relentlessly exploited by platforms, and, in that process, platforms have established both an ontological and economic reasoning for treating disruptive technologies with a yardstick based on 'exceptionalism'.

As has been noted earlier, the government has attempted to consolidate 29 labour laws into four codes: Code on Wages, 2019; the Industrial Relations Code, 2020; the Occupational Safety, Health and Working Conditions Code, 2020; and the Code on Social Security, 2020. With the exception of the Code on Social Security, the other codes have little on worker rights in the unorganised sector. In fact, these codes give the right to companies to hire and fire workers without government approval, make it difficult for unions to organise strike action (unions have to give 60-day notice) and enable women working on late-night shifts. While the GoI had hoped for the Codes to be ready for the financial year in April 2023, the possibility of a messy withdrawal of the four codes in an election year in 2024, like the withdrawal of the Farm Laws, has led to the stalling and delay in the implementation of these codes (Haq:2023). One of the key issues with these codes is that the rights of workers in the unorganised sector have been ignored – and this remains a critical issue in the context of an increase in gig workers and projected increases. As a report in the IDR (2020) website notes 'While the government claimed that the exercise of reform was aimed to extend coverage of statutory protection (including need based minimum wages, non-hazardous working conditions, universal social security entitlements) to unorganised sector workers, including new forms of work in the platform/gig economy, the reality is that the codes miserably fail to extend any form of social protection to the vast majority of informal sector workers including migrant workers, self-employed workers, home-based workers and other vulnerable groups'. While the Code on Social Security does include provisions related to insurance, provident fund, etc. for gig workers, it defines the unorganised sector as 'an enterprise owned by individuals or self-employed workers and engaged in the production or sale of goods or providing service of any kind whatsoever, and where the enterprise employs workers, the number of such workers is less than ten' 2 (85) (a definition that does not apply to gig platforms that typically contract out work to hundreds/thousands of workers) and then goes on to describe an unorganised worker 'as a self-employed, home-based or wage worker in the unorganised sector' 2 (86). While these distinctions may provide a necessary clarification of the distinct work and workers in this sector, they fail to emphasise the fact that all workers in the unorganised sector including platform-based gig workers face common challenges and deficits, especially in the matter of wages. So, it is odd that the GoI recognises their need for social security but not a minimum wage. In lieu of the constant foot-dragging by the GoI on the issue of provisioning rights for gig workers, the Indian Federation of App-based Transport Workers filed a public interest litigation in the Supreme Court on 20 September 2021 making a case for gig and platform workers to be classified as unorganised workers precisely because they could then fall under the purview of the Unorganised Workers Social Security Act, 2008 that offers statutory protection for social security benefits (see Tayal:2022).

Regulatory Woes

This exceptionalism has been profoundly shaped by the absence and lag in regulatory regimes related to digital platforms – the reality of 'catch-up' in a context characterised by constant innovation in the creation of transactional value. An example of catch-up in India is the introduction of the Cryptocurrency and Regulation of Official Digital Currency Bill, 2021 in the Lok Sabha that is yet to be passed. One reason for this lag is the position of the RBI which had recommended that cryptocurrencies be banned, although a Supreme Court of India ruling has contested this position (ET Now Digital, 2023). This ruling could well result in the RBI issuing an official digital currency in the not-too-distant future. In spite of this Bill being in limbo, Finance Minister Nirmala Sitharaman in the Union Budget 2022 presented a tax regime to deal with cryptocurrency. The measures include a 30 per cent tax on the transfer of digital assets, and investors in cryptocurrency are required to report profits and losses as part of their income. A finance ministry spokesperson Pankaj Chaudhry gave the following explanation for this delay in a parliamentary exchange in 2022 – 'Crypto assets are by definition borderless and require international collaboration to prevent regulatory arbitrage. Therefore, any legislation on the subject can be effective only with significant international collaboration on evaluation of the risks and benefits and evolution of common taxonomy and standards' (See Helms:2022). So, in other words, a tax regime for crypto has been established in India without the benefit of an explicit Bill. While there are practical reasons for establishing an ex-ante regime in lieu of formal legislation (as is the case in numerous jurisdictions around the world dealing with digital transactions), it nevertheless does highlight the gaps that exist in the GoI's regulation of digital assets and digital transactions. While there may well be arguments in favour of a temporary tax regime to deal with cryptocurrencies, the fact remains that such moves offer opportunities for creative forms of regulatory arbitrage and endless court battles resulting in a reputational stain on the GoI. There are also cases of the GoI blithely prosecuting citizens on the basis of redundant laws. One of the more egregious examples of the GoI's rather wilful disregard of legal niceties is its prosecution of hundreds of individuals for hate speech until late 2022 under Section 66A of the Information Technology Act, 2000 despite the fact that this Section had been struck down by the Supreme Court in 2015! (See The Economic Times:2022).

Bibliography

#startupindia, Startup Related Regulations and Notifications. Available at: https://www.startupindia.gov.in/content/sih/en/startupgov/regulatory_updates.html

Agarwal, P., Sonr, N. & Hegarty, S. (2023) Inside the Deadly Instant Loan App Scam That Blackmails with Nudes, *BBC*, October 8. Available at: https://www.bbc.com/news/world-asia-india-66964510

Athreya, V. (2021), Neoliberalism's Toll: Impacts on India's Peasants and Workers, *SP: The Bullet*, December 7. Available at: https://socialistproject.ca/2021/12/neoliberalism-toll-peasants-workers-india/

Barnes, T. (2015), *Informal Labour in Urban India: Three Cities, Three Journeys*, Routledge, London.

Basile, E. (2013), *Capitalist Development in India's Informal Economy*, Taylor and Francis, London.

Bhattacharya, S. and Kesar, S. (2020), Precarity and Development: Production and Labor Processes in the Informal Economy in India (387–408), *The Review of Radical Political Economics* 52(3).

Breman, J. (1996), *Footloose Labour Working in India's Informal Economy*, Cambridge University Press, Cambridge.

Code on Social Security (2020), Section2. Available at: https://www.indiacode.nic.in/show-data?actid=AC_CEN_6_0_00036_202036_1623221080799&sectionId=54026&sectionno=2&orderno=2

Coolman, F. (2021), Veni Vidi VC – The Backend of the Digital Economy and its Political Making (229–251), *Review of International Political Economy*, 30(1).

CreditVidya. How CredtVidya's SDK Works. Available at: https://www.creditvidya.com/how-it-works

D'Cruz, P. and Noronha, E. (2023), India's Platform Experience: A Site for the Commodification-Decommodification Dynamic (212–229), in Immanuel Ness (ed.) *Platform Labour and Global Logistics: A Research Companion*, Routledge, London & NY.

Dominic, J. and Gopalswamy, A. K. (2019), In the Venture Capital Market Liquid? Evidence from India (146–157), *Global Finance Journal*, 41.

Draft Compendium of Start-Up Specific Initiatives under Central Ministries, Government of India. Available at: https://www.startupindia.gov.in/content/dam/invest-india/Templates/public/Draft%20of%20Compendium%20of%20Startup%20Specific%20Initiatives%20(1).pdf

Dugar, P. and Basant, R. (2021), Antecedents of Stage-Wise Investment Preferences of Venture Capital and Private Equity Firms in India: An Empirical Exploration (264–289), *Journal of Emerging Market Finance*, 20(3).

ET Now Digital (2023), Bitcoin Inching Back towards 30,000? A Quick Look at the Indian Government's Policy on Crypto-Trading in Crypto, Tax on Cryptocurrency in India, *Times Now*, April 29. Available at: https://www.timesnownews.com/cryptonow/bitcoin-inching-back-towards-30000-a-quick-look-at-the-indian-governments-policy-on-crypto-trading-in-crypto-tax-on-cryptocurrency-in-india-article-99866678

Haq, Z. (2023), Implementation of 4 Labour Codes Stalled, *Hindustan Times*, May 8. Available at: https://www.hindustantimes.com/india-news/indias-sweeping-labour-code-implementation-stalled-until-2024-elections-101683485041321.html

Harriss-White, B. (2017), Rethinking Institutions: Innovation and Institutional Change in India's Formal Economy (1727–1755), *Modern Asian Studies*, 51(6).

Harriss-White, B. (2020), India's Informal Economy: Past, Present and Future (38–44) in Martha Chen and Francoise Carre (eds), *The Informal Economy Revisited: Examining the Past, Envisioning the Future*, Routledge, London.

Harriss-White, B. and Michelitti, L. (Eds.) (2019) *The Wild East: Criminal Political Economies in South Asia*, University College London Press, London.

Helms, K. (2022), Indian Government Updates Parliament on Cryptocurrency Bill and Investigations of Crypto Exchanges, *Bitcoin.com*, December 2022. Available at: https://news.bitcoin.com/indian-government-updates-parliament-on-cryptocurrency-bill-and-investigations-of-crypto-exchanges/

How the new labour laws deny workers their basic right (2020), IDR, September 25. Available at: https://idronline.org/denying-workers-their-rights-labour-law-reform-bill-codes/?amp&gclid=CjwKCAjw4ZWkBhA4EiwAVJXwqZ_qyUybttkZTS-PoOKpurvUZRrLCyPsiuY4WS0s16QZMcesDhW0QBoCNOEQAvD_BwE

Issues by Indian Companies, SEBI. (n.d.), Available at: https://www.sebi.gov.in/sebi_data/commondocs/subsection1_p.pdf

Jain, S. and Gabor, D. (2020), The Rise of Digital Financialisation: The Case of India (813–828), *New Political Economy*, 25 (5).

Jan, Breman (2012), *Footloose Labour: Working in India's Informal Economy*, Cambridge University Press, Cambridge.

Jayaram, K. (2022), Chasing Unicorns: India's Dreams of a Digital Economy, *The India Forum*, May 16. Available at: https://www.theindiaforum.in/article/chasing-unicorns-indias-dreams-digital-economy

Langley, P. and Leyshon, A. (2021), The Platform Political Economy of FinTech: Reintermediation, Consolidation and Capitalisation (376–388), *New Political Economy*, 26 (3).

Marjit, S. and Kar, S. (2011), *The Outsiders: Economic Reform and Informal Labour in a Developing Economy*, Oxford University Press, New Delhi.

Mehra, M. (2022), How Venture Capital Financing Work in India, *The Times of India*, October 31. Available at: https://timesofindia.indiatimes.com/blogs/voices/how-venture-capital-financing-work-in-india/

Mitra, A. (2014), Informal Economy in India: Persistence and Meagreness (216–231), *Agrarian South: Journal of Political Economy*, 4 (2). https://doi.org/10.1177/2277976015591415

Mukherjee, R. (2019), Jio Sparks Disruption 2.0: Infrastructural Imaginaries and Platform Eco-Systems in 'Digital India' (175–195), *Media, Culture & Society*, 41 (2).

Munck, R. (2013), The Precariat: A View from the South (747–762), *Third World Quarterly*, 35(5).

No citizens to be prosecuted under Section 66A IT Act: SC (2022), *The Economic Times*, October 12. Available at: https://economictimes.indiatimes.com/news/india/no-citizens-to-be-prosecuted-under-section-66a-it-act-sc/articleshow/94816298.cms?from=mdr

Objectives of E-Shram Portal. Available at: https://eshram.gov.in/e-shram-objectives

Poovanna, S. (2022), Everyone Loves an Indian Start-Up Success Story. Not Too Many Know that 2,000 Failed Last Year, *The Print*, December 8. Available at: https://theprint.in/india/everyone-loves-an-indian-start-up-success-story-not-too-many-know-that-2000-failed-last-year/1253302/

Rohit, K. V. N. (2023), Policy Violation: Google Takes Enforcement Action against 3500 Loan Apps on Play Store in India, *Deccan Herald*, April 2023. Available at: https://www.deccanherald.com/technology/policy-violation-google-takes-enforcement-action-on-3500-loan-apps-on-play-store-in-india-1213589.html

Sable, M. (2022), A Beginner's Guide to India's Venture Capital Landscape, *Going VC*, September22.Availableat:https://www.goingvc.com/post/a-beginners-guide-to-indias-venture-capital-landscape
Santos, A. C. (2022), Conceptualising State Financialisation: From the Core to the Periphery (142–154), *New Political Economy*, 28(1).
Singh, M. (2023a), Apple Purges Predatory Lending Apps in India Following Scrutiny, *TechCrunch*,July7.Availableat:https://techcrunch.com/2023/07/07/apple-purges-predatory-lending-apps-in-india-following-scrutiny/
Singh, M. (2023c), Invesco Cuts Swiggy Valuation by Half to $5.5 Billion, *TechCrunch*, May 8. Available at: https://techcrunch.com/2023/05/08/invesco-cuts-indian-food-delivery-giant-swiggys-valuation-to-5-5-billion/
Singh, V. (2023b) Explained: Why Are Foreign Funders No Longer Funding Start-Ups in India? *Wion*, April 19. Available at: https://www.wionews.com/business-economy/explained-why-are-foreign-investors-no-longer-funding-indian-startups-583991
Srnicek, N. (2017), *Platform Capitalism*, Polity, Cambridge/Malden.
Standing, G. (2011), *The Precariat: The New Dangerous Class*, Bloomsbury Academic, London.
Startupindia. Available at: https://www.startupindia.gov.in/
Surie, A. (2020), On Demand Platforms and Pricing: How Platforms Can Impact the Informal Urban Economy, Evidence from Bengaluru, India (83–100), *Work Organisation, Labour and Globalisation*, 14(1).
Tayal, H. (2022), Regulating the Gig Economy in India: How Secure Are Gig Workers? (1–10), *Supremo Amicus*, 28(January). Available at: https://supremoamicus.org/wp-content/uploads/2022/01/Haini-Tayal-.pdf
The 58 most active venture capital firms for startups in India, Inc42. (n.d.), Available at: https://inc42.com/wp-content/uploads/2018/09/eBook_Top-58-Venture_Capital_Firms_India.pdf
Unorganised Worker, Government of India, Ministry of Labour and Employment. Available at: https://labour.gov.in/unorganized-workers
Zider, B. (1998), How Venture Capital Works, *Harvard Business Review*, November-December. Available at: https://hbr.org/1998/11/how-venture-capital-works

4 AI, Machine Learning and Gig Workers in India

The GoI and AI

Referring to AI as a 'kinetic enabler', the MeitY, GoI, has described this area as significant and strategic, key to the development of applications supportive of a robust, people-centric digital ecosystem. In contrast, with global moves to regulate AI such as the EU's Artificial Intelligence Act, the GoI has decided to keep this sector free from regulation (Singh:2023) ostensibly to support innovation in the start-up industry and the harnessing of AI for better e-government services. The GoI has invested in the adoption of AI as a defining technology and strategic developmental priority and there are any number of mission-level national platforms such as the UPI that facilitate inter-bank financial transactions both peer to peer and person to merchant. In November 2022, there were nearly six billion transactions over UPI by 260 million users worth $121 billion. The GoI has invested in AI across all sectors that it is involved in notably in defence and security but also in the context of improving efficiencies and functionalities across different sectors such as the uses of language technology in the creation of vernacular language translations. Programmes such as the National Language Translation Mission, the Bhashini programme, the Samanantar AI tool and language tech start-ups such as Gnaani, Reverie and Devnagri help in the creation of language accessibility. The Samanantar AI Tool, for example, has helped Supreme Court orders and rulings to be translated into numerous vernacular languages (Elias:2023). The OECD AI Policy Observatory lists 23 AI-related investments made by the GoI – discussion papers, Centres of Excellence, policies and web portals. India is the present chair of the G20-related Global Partnership on Artificial Intelligence. The GoI believes that in lieu of specific legislation on AI, existing and proposed laws, accreditation and market rules could be used to 'regulate' the development of AI technologies and its implementation. For example, in the proposed DPDPB (2022), AI developers involved in using big data could be tasked as data fiduciaries to abide by ethical norms (Bordoloi:2023). While the draft Information Technology (Intermediaries Guidelines (Amendment) Rules), 2018 did seek out comments on the role of AI intermediaries, the government think tank NITI Aayog has brought out a discussion paper on AI

DOI: 10.4324/9781003491705-5

(Responsible AI:2022) and the Department of Telecommunications has established an AI standardisation committee. Explicit rules and norms related to the uses of AI in India are notably absent. Instead, the accent is on how AI can make a difference in strategic areas such as healthcare financial services, education, consumer and retail, public and utility services and agriculture (See Malhotra & Puhan:2022).

AI and DigiYatra

The discussion paper Responsible AI (2022) brought out by NITI Aayog highlights the efficiencies that are an outcome of automation. The example that is included in this paper of the Digital Yatra project (26–39) based on FRT highlights the benefits of Digi Yatra including lower congestion at airports, seamless, paperless and contactless passenger experience, lower operational costs and enhanced civil aviation capabilities (29–30). What is striking about this project is that it is aimed at effecting efficiencies at the expense of personnel employed by the Central Industrial Security Force (CISF) who have been involved in identity verification, travel documentation and carry-on luggage checks at all airports in India. While the paper does highlight the fact that travellers can opt out of automation and get CISF personnel to complete authentication checks manually, India really does not have a positive record on the matter of opt-out mechanisms. The original idea of the Aadhar ID card included opt-out mechanisms. Today, it has become the basis for all critical transactions linked to lives and livelihoods in India. 'Pertinently, the Digi Yatra programme is conceptualised as a purely voluntary mechanism, and therefore, at various stages, the Digi Yatra Policy sets out the alternative means in which the boarding process will operate for a passenger that does not opt-in to the Digi Yatra programme – namely, physical verification of their travel ID documents would continue to be done by CISF personnel at an airport. The current Digi Yatra process will, therefore, supplement human involvement at airports, and in time may be upscaled to all airports, with necessary legal frameworks in place' (29). There is another equally problematic issue – and this is the lackadaisical approach taken by the GoI to data security and data privacy. Sarasvati (2023), writing in the media portal MediaNama, highlights an exchange between Nikhil Pahwa of MediaNama and Union Minister of Civil Aviation Jyotiraditya Scindia on the security of the data collected by DigiYatra. Pahwa filed an RTI application that was refused but was informed that data is purged from the airport's system within 24 hours of the flight and that the data is shared only with the origin airport.

> The MoCA (Ministry of Civil Aviation) is planning to expand DigiYatra to other cities amid concerns related to the use of FRT – such as storage, sharing, and security of data and privacy of travellers – in the absence of a data protection regime. We have pointed out that it is unclear why one cannot seek information about the project under RTI, especially when the project has been circulated as a national policy since 2018.

There are no clear indications on DigiYatra's automatic deletion of data within 24 hours of a passenger taking a flight. The New Delhi–based Software Freedom Law Centre (SFLC) (2022:5) in a response to a report from NITI Aayog on AI deals explicitly with the need for DigiYatra to have safeguards in place that will protect passenger privacy.

> Principals i.e., users are made fully aware of the processes and entities which will be utilizing their personal data. In light of this, the form of consent which should be taken from data principals upon availing the services of Digi Yatra must be 'informed explicit consent'. This would require the Data Fiduciary to explain unambiguously to the Data Principal all the uses and vulnerabilities their data may be exposed to in a manner understandable by the data principal, and take explicit consent after such information has been communicated.

While the SFLC's recommendations are robust, there is little evidence that civil society–based interventions on AI or for that matter other social and technology-related concerns are taken seriously by the government. The data breach of customers of Telegram and their COVID Vaccine Intelligence Network (CoWIN) status in June 2023 is of concern precisely because this network is integrated into the health apps Aarogya Setu and UMANG, as the latter is a single platform that can be used by Indian citizens to access e-government services across states in India (Perappadan:2023). The breach exposed details of the person's ID number including Aadhar, passport or PAN card, gender, date of birth, etc.

National Strategy for AI

The National Strategy for AI (2018) also published by NITI Aayog is similarly optimistic about its deployment across all productive sectors in India including healthcare, education and agriculture. This document is clearly imprinted on every page with the GoI's commitment to AI and neoliberal growth through public–private partnerships with Big Tech companies including IBM, Microsoft and accounting firms such as Accenture. The section on Precision Agriculture is based on a report by Accenture extols the values of smartphone-based uses of agricultural data generated by sensors, autonomous tractors and drones. Here again, while there is no mention of its impact on labour, there is an implicit belief that adoption will result in greater growth, productivity and efficiencies in this sector. While there is an entire section on Ethics, Privacy, Security and Artificial Intelligence (85–89), there is very little on how AI-based data will be made secure, privacy linked to personal data and how innovations in the following areas will ensure a rights-based #AIforALL. 'a) object detection in images or video streams; b) conversational smart chatbots (text and speech); c) speech-to-text and text-to-speech; d) assistive diagnostic solutions; e) language recognition and transcription; f) contextual data mining to discover complex patterns; g) price optimisation; h) data collection, curation and annotation for specific business use; i) supply and demand forecasting; and j) server, app and web uptime/downtime prediction'(National Strategy for AI:2018, 81) – all key areas that are fundamental to the functioning of platforms in the gig economy. Vidushi Marda (2018:4), in a critical article on India's AI policy, has argued that much of the official policy on AI in India is ad hoc, created by different government ministries and falls short of comprehensiveness. AI is treated fundamentally as an economic lever that will unlock India's potential as a superpower in digital innovation. As Marda has observed

> it fails to meaningfully address the ethical, social and technical limitations that undergird the use of AI technologies. Commenting on a government task force on AI, Marda notes that while this task force "touches upon concerns of data privacy, it fails to consider the proclivity of data-driven decision-making to embed and exacerbate historical bias and discrimination. The potential for well-intentioned algorithmic systems to have disproportionate consequences on vulnerable and marginalised communities is also left unconsidered.
>
> (4)

While the GoI is committed to an inclusive AI on paper, it is unclear whether the deployments of AI will accentuate unemployment in a country in which the availability of labour is a core strength. The reality of AI making some jobs redundant is reflected in the announcement by the UK-based British Telecom that out of the 40,000 job cuts envisaged by 2030, 10,000 will be replaced by AI-related technology (Espiner:2023).

In 2022, India's service economy contributed over 50 per cent to India's GDP, was the largest recipient of FDI flows worth $16.7 billion and is a major contributor to India's $3.5 trillion economy. In a perverse way, pandemic-related shutdowns in the previous two years contributed to a major growth in e-commerce, to a growth in start-ups and accelerated the government's commitment to developing India Stack and public digital infrastructures. This growth, however, belies the realities of uneven growth, growing income disparities and employment that is concentrated in various sectors linked to the gig economy including agriculture, construction and of late, digital platforms. As Duvisac (2022:362) has observed, labour relations in post-Independent India have been characterised by agriculture and by informality in work both in the urban and rural sectors. There have been high rates of growth in informal work at the expense of jobs in the formal economy linked to both the private and public sectors – a reality that highlights the employment crisis in India. The mismatch between jobs and applications is highlighted in the fact that in March 2018, after a three-year recruitment hiatus, the Railway Recruitment Board circulated advertisements for 100,000 jobs for which there were 23 million applications. In the same year, 200,000 people in Mumbai applied for 1137 jobs as constables in the Mumbai police. In 2015,

386 clerical jobs at a local secretariat in Uttar Pradesh received 2.3 million applications (Hemrajani:2018) while in 2023 there were 35,000 applicants including those with PG degrees who applied for a one-year contract as gardeners and snake catchers in the forest department in West Bengal (ENS:2023). While the security of a government job is a major factor, this discrepancy between jobs and applicant numbers is a persistent reality in every state in India. It is in this context that we need to evaluate automation.

Automation and Unemployment

The enthusiastic embrace of automation in India to replace human labour in the pursuit of capitalist efficiencies seems rather misplaced in a situation characterised by high unemployment across multiple sectors. While some automation makes sense in industry and manufacturing where robots can be used to replace people working with dangerous chemicals, it does not make sense to just replace jobs as, for example, those in check-in counters with automated self-check-in at some Indian airports or in the so-called smart cities that seem resistant to outsiders who have been dispensed with in return for smart technologies and the car industry where automation has replaced workers. The present government's technocratic embrace of the digital at the expense of investing in the ordinary lives and livelihoods of people does seem myopic and the result of its inability to understand the depth of India's current unemployment crisis. The enthusiastic embrace of the gig economy is arguably just another example of this myopia. Pritchett (2023) writing in the journal *Foreign Affairs* highlights the ludicrousness of capitalist efficiencies in the context of the USA that has far less problems related to unemployment than in India.

> Automation is often a solution in search of a problem. It is a choice people have made, not an inevitability and certainly not a necessity. For instance, the United States faces a scarcity of truck drivers. The American Trucking Association has estimated that in 2021 there were 80,000 fewer drivers than the total needed and that, given the age of current drivers, over a million new ones will have to be recruited in the coming decade. To deal with this deficit, many tech moguls, including Amazon founder Jeff Bezos, have invested in the research and development of self-driving vehicles, technology that would reduce the demand for drivers. For Bezos, such technology makes corporate financial sense; Amazon relies on low shipping costs to keep its prices down. But it does not make wider economic sense because millions of people would be happy to drive trucks in the United States-they just need to be allowed to work in the country.

While there has been the development of organised labour in the manufacturing sector, employment in agricultural work has remained more or less unorganised and continues to account for the bulk of workers in India. The unemployment crisis has been especially acute in the so-called 'Bimaru' states (Bihar, Madhya Pradesh, Rajasthan and Uttar Pradesh) and in the states in North East India – and this constant stream of migrant labour to the rest of India in the domestic help and other sectors has led to a growth in intermediation provided by a range of digital platforms. Tandon and Rathi (2022:2–5) in an article on domestic workers and the gig economy in India have observed that as against the exploitation of migrant workers by traditional placement agencies, *marketplace platforms* (Helper4u, Helpers Near Me, Babajob by Quikr and Rozgarkhoj), *digital platform agencies* (Domestic For You, Housmaid, HomeDruid, Kaamwalibais and Gharelu Help) and *on-demand platforms* (Urban Company, Housejoy, CleanPro, Mr. Right, Creo Jobs, UnplanGo, Broomberg, Quikr and Cleansy) guaranteed a steady income to domestic workers although this is at the expense of other precarities including increased surveillance and being subject to the vagaries of algorithmic management.

Platforms and Regulatory Arbitrage

The key to the success of platforms and the ecosystem of start-ups and the gig economy is the 'regulatory arbitrage' that platforms have been able to negotiate through legal means. In a seminal article on this subject, Victor Fleischer (2010:2) describes it as follows 'Regulatory arbitrage exploits the gap between the economic substance of a transaction and its legal or regulatory treatment, taking advantage of the legal system's intrinsically limited ability to attach formal labels that track the economics of transactions with sufficient precision'. In other words, in the absence of regulatory regimes and the inability to clearly define digitally mediated transactions and to assign such transactions economic value, lawyers have argued the case for the singularity and the disruptive innovativeness of platforms in the creation of economic value while creatively arguing in favour of the new conditions of labour, work, compensation and rights that are unmoored from any legal precedents and universally applicable standards. Algorithmic management offers an alibi for employers to attribute what really are manipulations in rankings, work assignment, work optimisation and compensation to the vagaries of the digital sublime thus sidestepping platform investments in algorithmic management as a form of worker control.

While banks in particular have had a dubious reputation for regulatory arbitrage – for example, HSBC's involvement in money laundering and evidence of many thousands of cases of corporate and individual tax evasion highlighted in the Pandora and Panama exposes by the International Consortium of Investigative Journalists (ICIJ), leading digital platforms and search and sociality operations such as Apple, Google, Amazon and Facebook and disruptive innovators such as Uber, Swiggy and other platforms in India and elsewhere have used their legal, political and economic capital to quite relentlessly use regulatory arbitrage to their advantage. It is only over the last decade that national and state governments (USA and California, Germany, France and India) and regional entities such as the European Union have contested the power of the platforms by enforcing anti-trust procedures, shutting down their options for tax evasion and combating the anti-competitive and monopolising tendencies of all the major global digital platforms. These attempts at the harmonisation of laws and exploring global solutions such as the Organisation for Economic Co-Operation and Development's/G20's Inclusive Framework on Base Erosion and Profit Sharing (BEPS) that prescribes a 15 per cent minimum tax for multinational enterprises which came into force in December 2021 (OECD Releases Two Pillar Model…) are few and far between. Harmonisation is often difficult to achieve precisely because multinational companies, for example, Big Tech companies are typically involved in lobbying for favourable treatment in the jurisdictions that they operate in.

Kristelia Garcia (2019:208), in an article in the *California Law Review*, refers to two types of regulatory arbitrage – ontological and technological often used by Big Tech companies.

> Ontological regulatory arbitrage allows an entity to either switch to, or away from, a particular label, depending on whether it aims to avoid, or to bring itself under, a particular regulation. An example is when a business decides to incorporate offshore to avoid paying domestic taxes. Technological regulatory arbitrage entails coding, designing, or otherwise innovating around a regulation so as to avoid its purview altogether.

Pollman (2019:8) highlights jurisdictional arbitrage – companies taking advantage of legal differences in different countries, for example, low taxes in Ireland as opposed to paying higher taxes in Germany and categorical arbitrage that refers to legal differences between 'the treatment of two types of activity or products that are functionally similar', for example, between traditional gig workers in the construction industry in India who have some protection versus gig workers in the platform economy who, for the most part, continue to not enjoy any rights whatsoever.

Swiggy and Algorithmic Management in Practice

As a technologically challenged person, I had found it hard to figure out the intricacies of machine learning until I came across a very clearly explained video on Youtube (https://www.youtube.com/watch?v=INU555Uo1pE) hosted by Sachin Manji on the way in which Swiggy employed data science to ensure that its 'delivery executives' (a.k.a. delivery partners) complied with the company's mask policy while making food deliveries in the context of the COVID pandemic in India. Swiggy and Zomato are the two market leaders in food delivery in India. Manji explained the involvement of Swiggy's partner restaurants (195,000 in FY 2022 serviced by 150,000 delivery partners, Menghani:2022) in taking photographs of before and after delivery selfies taken by delivery partners that contributed to the creation of a 10,000 picture databank on each delivery partner. These photographs were annotated by a machine learning algorithm – the Convolutional Neural Network that used Retina Face and Feature Pyramid Networks to create a mask detection feature that was launched in its delivery app. This feature was used to detect the use of non-approved masks, unapproved masks or no masks. There were initially glitches with the object detection algorithm that was based on object occlusion. This algorithm recognition process began by recognising eyes although if you used your palm to cover your nose and mouth it could not detect this substitution of one's palm for a mask. However, this has since been resolved and the feature now has added surveillance features including checking the temperature of the delivery partner and detecting whether he (there are very few women in this industry) is wearing the right, Swiggy gear.

At a very basic level, masking is an important protective measure that restricts person-to-person transmission of COVID and in that sense saves lives and slows down its transmission. So the requirement to wear a mask is common sense. However, delivery partners were frontline workers during the pandemic delivering an essential service and their compliance was arguably not matched by the compliance of customers or the delivery environment that reflected gradations of compliance on the matter of mask-wearing. Sazzad Parwez (2022:7) in an article on delivery workers and precarity during COVID cites a delivery partner whom he had interviewed "Customers shout and tell us to deliver and ask us to leave food at the door, even though we are supposed to make contactless delivery. We are forced to make delivery at doorsteps bearing the risk of contamination. Further, a few days ago, a customer complaint against me as I asked him to come to the gate and collect the food." This contractual blurriness that is probably replicated in terms and conditions for other types of gig work suggests that the term 'precarity' that is often used to describe gig work is the right term. The entire system is built on the precarity of workers who can be shaped, nudged, cajoled or threatened to fall in line or experience precarity. This intensely managed, algorithmic management has also been described as 'algorithmic despotism' (See Griesbach, et al.: 2019:2). Bhattacharya (2022) in an article on Zomato Instant refers to the algorithmic insanity in actioning food deliveries in 10 minutes in the context of road conditions, the inaccuracy of Google maps, delays in food preparation, distances, for example, food delivery to gated communities who live on large estates and the always present threat of road accidents. While the COVID 19 mask issue can be seen to be a one-off compliance related project, food platforms such as Swiggy and Zomato invest primarily in algorithms that expand delivery efficiencies (Just in Time, Next Order Assignment and Batching), food recommendations for users, chatbots and voice recognition among other services. From a rights perspective, algorithms that are used to create delivery efficiencies are most problematic as they are focused on the actioning of faster deliveries focused on delivery partners whose time-based delivery schedule is algorithmically driven. The risk in the context of food delivery platform competition is investments in people as automatons who are completely at the mercy of time-specified delivery routines and delays that can incur penalties.

This focused use of FRTs by Swiggy and algorithms to detect mask-wearing that is based on both self-surveillance and surveillance at food pick-up outlets is possible primarily because of the status of the delivery partners who have no rights to speak of and are in a contractual relationship that is very elastic and vague. Swiggy's terms and conditions specify that they are strictly 'intermediaries' and that their pick-up and delivery partners (PDPs) act out a contractual service every time they complete a delivery job. *'PDPs are individual entrepreneurs engaged with Swiggy on a voluntary, non-exclusive and principal to principal basis to provide aforementioned services for service fee. PDPs are independent contractors and are free to determine their timings of work. Swiggy does not exercise control on the PDPs and the relationship between the PDPs and Swiggy is not that of an agent and principal or employee and employer'*. Under the section Use of Platform and Services, Swiggy makes it clear that when the PDP is involved in completing the order, the PDP is not contractually bound to Swiggy but the Merchants/Buyers 'Upon acceptance of any Order or Task by the PDPs, the pickup and delivery services or Task completion services (as the case may be) undertaken by him/her, shall constitute a separate contract for services between Merchants/Buyers and PDPs. Swiggy shall not be responsible for the services provided by PDP to Merchants/Buyers through the Platform'. So it would seem that Swiggy's algorithmic investments are ensuring the PDPs' delivery efficiencies and the calculation of compensation for services rendered that may change from time to time. It is also interesting that the terms and conditions highlight the fact that the PDPs are not paid by the platform as per the terms and conditions but by the buyers or merchants. 'For the pickup and delivery services and completing the Tasks, PDPs may charge the users of the Platform (Buyers or Merchants), a service fee (inclusive of applicable taxes whenever not expressly mentioned) determined on the basis of various factors including but not limited to distance covered, time taken, demand for delivery services/Tasks, real time analysis of traffic and weather conditions, seasonal peaks or such other parameters as may be determined from time to time'. What this wording clearly indicates is the contractual distance between Swiggy and the PDPs employed by them. While Swiggy does for all practical purposes, compensate PDPs through direct transfers for each task completed, the legal wording suggests that the PDP charges a service fee to Buyers and Merchants for services rendered. So such legalese ensures that Swiggy's contractual obligations to PDPs are at the bare minimum precisely because the delivery executive really has the status of an 'errand boy'. This hands-off approach highlighted in Swiggy's terms and conditions does stretch legal credulousness and highlights the fact that platforms have created their own in-house policies in the context of legal precedence and the lack of legal clarity over self-descriptors used by platforms – intermediary, logistics company and facilitator. It is only over the last few years that these descriptors have been called out. Kashyap (2022) refers to a case filed by one Mohit Gupta against Swiggy for not delivering food within the stipulated 30 minutes. Swiggy's counsel argued that the platform did not have any liabilities for the non-delivery of food in the stipulated time 'Swiggy's counsel stated that Swiggy is neither the seller of food or beverages nor delivers the food or beverages on its own. Therefore, it cannot be held liable for any deficiency arising out of the non-delivery of order either by the restaurant or the delivery partner. In essence, the food delivery major stated that it was only there to facilitate placing orders with restaurants. This claim was rejected by the commission' who took the view that Swiggy simply had to fulfil its contract with the restaurant and the PDP (despite the company trying to obscure the meaning of the term 'contract' in their terms and conditions). In Australia, the News Media and Digital Platforms Mandatory Bargaining Code, 2021 has basically forced Google and Facebook to confront the reality that they are not just 'intermediaries' but 'publishers' in their own right and compensate legacy media for content replicated on platforms (See Meaker, 2022). In other words, platforms have consistently established misleading contracts based on the misclassification and obfuscation of terms of service. The regulatory inertia that accompanied the growth of the platform economy enabled platforms to create their own rules and self-regulation, although this, as was to be expected, merely reinforced their control over the labour they had contracted. The algorithmic management of these workers adds another layer of complexity in addition to the fact that it is often the case that platforms are involved typically in de-centralised operations with minimal brick-and-mortar presence in the cities that they operate in. So, the hotline that workers are given is often to administrators located in one of the major cities in India or worse to bots that provide impersonal, automated information in response to queries, complaints and requests.

So arguably, Swiggy's entire algorithmically driven structure is built on a legal framework that is at odds with interpretations of public law. In this structure, workers are dispensable and treated as automated machines that are shorn of their human dignity. Satisfying customers, on the other hand, is the primary goal of food delivery and ride-hailing platforms. Algorithmically driven ratings that are totally outside the control of delivery partners and drivers are controlled by customers who do not have to justify the rating that they have given. So ratings are more than just a means to discipline platform workers. It is an instrument that is inherently coercive. This is especially problematic in countries such as India that are inherently hierarchical and where caste, colour, religion and other markers of identity can and do play a role in reinforcing divides and power structures. As Naraharisetty (2021) has observed

> The final nail in the coffin of a worker's autonomy, then, is that the algorithms don't filter out the biases and discrimination of users. In an exceedingly casteist, classist social structure like India's, discrimination and bias often work in quiet ways, and this gets magnified on gig platforms: customers have the power to get away with rating someone badly

solely on the basis of prejudice. The effects of the discrimination don't end there: "The worker in the marginalized group is more likely to get kicked out of the platform just because of the amplification of the discrimination".

Marx and Piecemeal Work

The business model that runs the gig economy is based on compensation for piecemeal work and the algorithms facilitate piecemeal work and piecemeal compensations for work. 'The movement from hourly rates to piece rate – or rather to an entirely piece rate arrangement – is a further method through which Deliveroo is shifting the risk of the business model onto workers. In the absence of physical supervision, Deliveroo has developed methods to encourage workers to make timely deliveries. The piece rate means that workers can measure the relationship between their own performance and pay: the more they deliver over a shift, the more money they make' (Woodcock:2020:83).

In other words, algorithms are responsible for structuring both work and wages in the platform economy. Marx, in Capital Volume 1, Chapter Twenty-One, made an attempt to understand piecemeal wages, its conditions and the consequences in the context of understanding wages in general. In a characteristically critical manner, he highlights the role played by 'parasites' (read platform intermediaries) in the exploitation of labour. '.....piece wages facilitate the interposition of parasites between the capitalist and the wage-labourer, the "sub-letting of labour."' The gain of these middlemen comes entirely from the difference between the labour price which the capitalist pays and the part of that price which they actually allow to reach the labourer". Marx follows on by making a very prescient and astute observation related to piece labour that can be applied to an understanding of the labouring of gig workers.

> "Given piece-wage, it is naturally the personal interest of the labourer to strain his labour-power as intensely as possible; this enables the capitalist to raise more easily the normal degree of intensity of labour. It is moreover now the personal interest of the labourer to lengthen the working-day, since with it his daily or weekly wages rise. This gradually brings on a reaction like that already described in time-wages, without reckoning that the prolongation of the working-day, even if the piece wage remains constant, includes of necessity a fall in the price of the labour"

This is exactly the situation in the global platform economy where rewards for longer hours at work facilitate greater work intensity and falling wages that have become the norm. A report written for the NGO, Worker Information Exchange, by Cansu Safak and James Farrar (2021), on Uber and other gig economy workers in the UK – *Managed by Bots: Data-Driven Exploitation in the Gig Economy* includes a forthright critique of platforms that only divulge data on their algorithmic management practices after they are forced to do so, post-litigation. As Safak and Farrar (2021:4) note, after having 'processed more than 500 subject access requests over the last eight months on behalf of workers at Amazon Flex, Bolt, Deliveroo, Free Now, Just Eat, Ola and Uber. The persistent and widespread lack of compliance with data protection laws has hindered worker access to data and yielded almost no meaningful algorithmic transparency over critical worker management functions such as recruitment, performance management, work allocation and dismissals. The obfuscation and general lack of compliance has prevented us from reaching scale with a worker data trust. Instead, we have had to turn to strategic litigation across international boundaries to help workers once again secure their workplace rights'. Algorithmic management is used in the planning and organising of work, the allocation of tasks, the control and monitoring of workers and the evaluation and disciplining of workers (Rani, Dhir & Gobel:2022).

The Ubiquity of Facial Recognition Technologies

Jamie Woodcock (2020) in an article on the algorithmic panopticon at a food delivery platform, Deliveroo, makes the point that such systems of measurement and control evolved in the factory system and were perfected in the call centre economy where workers were/are continuously monitored. The techniques may have changed from the surveillance of the production of tangible goods and services to that of intangibles although the objective remains the same – to increase productivity by using systems of rewarding, disciplining and punishing although arguably these automated modes are more exploitative as they occur largely in a context in which gig workers have little or no rights. Moves by Swiggy's Applied Research Team to partner with the Indian Institute of Technology, Jodhpur to create a facial recognition system specifically to help with the background verification of its delivery partners (help fraud detection, impersonation, etc) goes against NITI Aayog's pronouncements on Privacy by Design although such projects are possible precisely because gig workers have little or no legal rights (Sanzgiri:2022). Uber's use of 'Real Time ID Checks' based on the upload of selfies by its 600,000 drivers in India has been a verification nightmare for many drivers who have had to face being blocked out of the system because of the failures of facial recognition (Bansal:2022b). NITI Aayog (2022:1–86) paper 'Responsible AI for All: Adopting the Framework – A use case approach on Facial Recognition Technology' in Annex 3 (57–63) highlights seven design-based risks 'Inaccuracy due to technical factors, inaccuracy due to bias or underrepresentation, inaccuracy due to the lack of training of human agents, inaccuracy due to deliberate tweaks in images, security risks due to data breaches and unauthorised access, accountability, legal liability and grievance redressal, opaque nature of FRT systems'. While the paper includes recommendations for governing legislation and policy, developers and vendors of FRT systems, procurement and impacted customers with a clear onus on the need for transparency, explanatory accuracy of design principles, clarity in terms of its implementation in FRT systems, inclusionary and non-discriminatory nature and privacy, the report is primarily directed towards FRT systems in public projects and in the context of the continuing impasse over privacy legislation, just another report, at least for the moment. The GoI does have a reputation for implementing large-scale public-oriented digital projects without necessary safeguards in place such as basic privacy and personal data protection laws. The country still lacks a data governance framework for the collection and retention of sensitive personal data such as at airports. While the GoI has invested in 125 FRT systems (Thathoo:2022), there is concern over the low threshold for facial recognition scans conducted by the police in New Delhi and Telangana where 80 per cent accuracy is considered a positive match that will be corroborated with other evidence (Bansal:2022a). More than 1000 farmers who protested at a farmer's rally in New Delhi in 2021 were arrested by the police who used an FRT system called Trinetra – one example among many protestors being tracked for their 'anti-national' activities on the basis of arbitrary and manufactured interpretations of nationalism and patriotism (Murgia:2022). In the context of lax laws, FRT uses in the commercial sector to monitor emotion recognition, fraud detection, impersonation, attendance tracking and monitoring, security and surveillance and worker compliance are bound to be compromised because 'safety nets' are a secondary priority in the context of the government's avowed ambitions to become a digital superpower and a trillion-dollar economy. So it would seem that in the context of a growth-at-all-costs approach, civil liberties, privacy and frameworks that facilitate judicious approaches to algorithmic management are destined to be of secondary concern, at least for the moment. Delivery partners, ride share drivers along with many welfare recipients in India have complained of the failures of biometric identification and its consequences on lives that already are on the edge. While Aadhar has certainly contributed towards inclusivity, the fact that Aadhar authentication is now mandatory for access to a whole range of services from the filing of tax returns to the booking of railway tickets highlights mission creep. This surge in biometric-based transactions has also led to evidence of rather large failures, for example, a 49 per cent failure to match rate in Jharkhand and 37 per cent in Rajasthan (Dixon:2017, 547). Jain and Parsheera (2021) in an audit of four facial processing systems in India – Microsoft Azure's Face, Amazon's Rekognition, Face++ and FaceX (across face recognition, gender and age) – of the images of 32,184 electoral candidates culled from the Election Commission of India (ECI) in 2019–2020 highlight error rates across the three areas including facial recognition – 'The four tools differ significantly in their ability to detect faces. Amazon performed the best, with an error rate of 0.05% while Microsoft performed the worst, reporting an error rate of 3.17%. To contextualise this in terms of numbers, out of the 32,184 persons in the dataset, Microsoft was unable to accurately detect the faces of a little over a thousand persons. This figure was similarly high for FaceX, which failed to detect 865 of the faces. While significant in themselves, the implications of these figures become all the more relevant when we take into account a population size of over 1.34 billion people, with many individuals being forced to encounter multiple facial processing projects' (12).

On Algorithmic Arbitrariness

Algorithmic management is not just a feature of food delivery and ride platforms but has become increasingly essential to the functioning of contemporary, transactional and capitalist society (See Indian Artificial Intelligence Stack, 2020). Algorithmic management is the basis for India Stack although, for the most part, it is focused on the delivery of efficiencies and entitlements on the basis of biometric identification. However, even in the case of India Stack, there is the potential for administrative management and control and cases of many beneficiaries experiencing algorithmic arbitrariness, of those who have experienced difficulties in redressing the situation precisely because of the centralised nature of its architectures and the blurriness related to accessing customer service within such a gargantuan network (See Dreze et al.: 2017). Chaudhuri (2022:898) in an article on programmed welfare in India highlights a new set of intermediaries that citizens have to negotiate with in the case of algorithmic exclusions 'enrolment agents, seeding agents and data entry operators in government offices'. Arguably, India Stack is the apotheosis of attempts by the GoI to achieve perfect, technological governance of its citizens via digital transactions. Governance in India today is managed through technological mediation and algorithmic fiat precisely because it involves the transfers of digitised finance in a country that has stated its desire to become a cashless society in which citizens have become its customers. In the case of India Stack too, as Dattani (2019:416) has observed, the corporate imprint is unmistakeable, the 'weaving of corporate into government' resulting in personal data (in the absence of privacy laws) falling into the hands of the state and the corporate sector. There are a number of issues related to AI in India that require resolution. 1) In the absence of laws that specifically facilitate citizen contestation of automated decision-making and AI, it is difficult for ordinary people to get redress when the system fails or when they are wrongfully denied access to services and entitlements. In other words, there is a need for fairness and transparency precisely because digital transactions have begun to shape the lives of the majority of Indian citizens who are beneficiaries of India Stack. 2) In a context in which the vision of India is being advanced through public–private partnerships, there is a lack of clarity with respect to the ownership and security of the billions of transactional data that are generated on a daily basis. 3) Food delivery, ride and job platforms use data generated by their 'workers' to create algorithmic solutions to the need for better targeted and efficient work processes that earn companies better profits. In the public sector, the outsourcing of digital solutions to private vendors raises a key issue that Joshi (2021) has identified. Since 'Most applications of AI in administration are through the procurement of AI technologies from private vendors—whether the data that is used or the algorithmic processes and software. In doing so, agencies are outsourcing not only the creation of technologies, but also the process of making policy decisions themselves, to private vendors, who are currently not guided by any obligations to make technologies whose outcomes are fair, transparent, accountable and participatory in ways that conform to democratic values'. In other words, the lack of explicit standards, guidelines, policies, rules and responsibilities related to data governance has resulted in data governmentalities. 4) The need to monitor the uses of algorithms in the manipulation of consumer choices and the auditing of algorithms (See Sivasubramaniam:2021).

Algorithmic management is also based on the gamification of the platform–delivery and platform/customer relationships. Broadly speaking, gamification refers to both the 'gaming' of the system and the creation of expectations and rewards that act as a bait to lure partners and drivers but that are programmed/tweaked resulting in lower orders per delivery partner and lower rewards and the incorporation of game design features into driver apps and games into customer apps. Delivery partners and ride share riders are often enticed by the prospect of independent, flexible work and orders and rides that in the beginning are plentiful. Over time, this surfeit often declines – and in the context of an excess of delivery partners in a given area and intense competition between food delivery platforms, orders become less regular, ratings become inconsistent and partners are pushed to work harder to earn minimum wages (Sharma:2021). Another issue that has merited research attention (See Vasudevan & Chan:2020 and de Oliveira: 2020) is the incorporation of game design into the Uber driver app ostensibly to improve driver interaction and improve their overall experience (after negative feedback) by making work fun and challenging." "Games deliver an instantaneous, visceral experience of success and reward, and they are increasingly used in the workplace to promote emotional engagement with the work process to increase workers' psychological investment in completing otherwise uninspiring tasks and to influence, or 'nudge', workers' behaviour" (Mason:2018). Uber has 'experimented with videogame techniques, graphics and no-cash rewards' (Scheiber:2017) and interfaces that nudge/induce drivers to attain goals that enhance personal achievement. When drivers are involved in income goals, they get into a 'ludic loop' (a feeling associated with the stacking blocks game Tetris) and they get psychologically prepped into more driving in income achievement stakes that are like playing pinball/pokie machines. They are also motivated to earn virtual badges for excellent work and take part in 'binge driving' – accept a continuous stream of new work even before completion of the previous job. These games come with an earnings tracker on top so that drivers can see how much they have earned. A constant streaming of messages, texts and pop-ups alert drivers of how close they are to their target, that for the most part remains elusive. Gamification is also used to engage with customers and earn their loyalty. Such gamification strategies have been used previously by Swiggy. Swiggy had incorporated a spinning wheel for first-time users to play after they had ordered which would enable them to get cash back on their next order. This was a major success and, as a result, the verb 'Swiggy It' became part of a popular food-ordering parlance. In 2020, both Swiggy and Zomato were forced to withdraw their Indian Premier League (IPL) cashback games on their customer apps after Google complained that this violated Google Play Store rules related to gambling (Bhalla: 2020). Google's moves that affected Paytm (India's most valuable app), Swiggy, Zomato and other start-ups were contested by these startups who argued that such features were often launched during festivals and sporting events and against Google's control over and policing of such features. Google's monopolistic control over the smartphone market in India and attempts to levy a 30 per cent cut on revenues earned through app-related payments have led to attempts by these start-ups to establish an alternative app store (Singh:2020).

While the GoI has explicitly invested in AI at a variety of levels, there are concerns with its haste to implement AI-based solutions in its attempt to become a global leader. In the absence of any regulations on AI, privacy and the rights of workers in the gig economy, it would seem that both the GoI and the corporate sector have had unrestricted opportunities to innovate solutions, some that may be well-intentioned but fall short on the critical matter of data security. The use of FRT across sectors in India by both the central and state governments including policing and verification used by banks can result in serious violations of privacy, wrongful identification and denial of services. The sharing of data between the government and corporates and the use of corporate data and cloud centres by the central and state governments in India to store data on citizens are issues because the majority of citizens are not aware of how their personal data or the data that they generate is used and for what purposes. There simply is a huge gap between the reports and projections on the benefits of AI prepared by the government often with the help of corporate groups such as Accenture and ground realities that require non-tech solutions.

Bibliography

Bansal, V. (2022a), The Low Threshold for Face Recognition in New Delhi, *Wired*, August 21. Available at: https://www.wired.com/story/delhi-police-facial-recognition/

Bansal, V. (2022b), Uber's Facial Recognition Is Locking Indian Drivers Out of Their Accounts, *MIT Technology Review*, December 6. Available at: https://www.technologyreview.com/2022/12/06/1064287/ubers-facial-recognition-is-locking-indian-drivers-out-of-their-accounts/

Bhalla, T. (2020), Zomato and Swiggy Pause Gamification on App After Googel Notice, Mint, September 30. Available at: https://www.livemint.com/companies/news/zomato-and-swiggy-pause-gamification-on-app-after-google-notice-11601483995638.html

Bhattacharya, A. (2022), Zomato's Instant Delivery Could Crush Its Drivers, *Quartz*, March 23. Available at: https://qz.com/india/2145700/instant-delivery-algorithms-aside-what-about-the-humans-of-zomato#:~:text=Zomato%20Instant%2C%20which%20promises%20to,With%20algorithms

Bordoloi, P. (2023), India Backs Off on AI Regulation. But Why?, *AnalyticsIndiamag*, April 10. Available at: https://analyticsindiamag.com/india-backs-off-on-ai-regulation-but-why/

Chaudhuri, B. (2022), Programmed Welfare: An Ethnographic Account of Algorithmic Practices in the Public Distribution System in India (887–902), *New Media & Society* 24(4).

Dattani, K. (2019), 'Governtrepreneurism' for Good Governance: The Case of Aadhar and the Indian Stack (411–418), *Area*, 52.

De Oliveira, R. C. (2020), Gamification and Uberised Work in Application Companies (1–10), *RAE (Journal of Business Management)*, 61(4). Available at: https://www.scielo.br/j/rae/a/yN9ZkXFfcNwyxg8T9mQxGbL/?lang=en&format=pdf

Dixon, P. (2017), A Failure to "Do No Harm" – India's Aadhar Biometric Program and its Inability to Protect Privacy in Relation to Measures in Europe and the USA (539–567), *Health Technology*, 7.

Dreze, J., Khalid, N., Khera, R. and Somanchi, A. (2017), Aadhar and food security in Jharkhand: Pain without gain (50–59), *Economic and Political Weekly* 52 (50).

Duvisic, S. (2022) The Unfulfilled Promise of Gig Work: Unpacking Informality and Gig Work in India (361–373), in Immanuel Ness (Ed.) *The Routledge Handbook of the Gig Economy*, Routledge, London.

Elias, J. (2023), AI for All: How India Is Carving Its Own Path in the Global AI Race, OECD.AI Policy Observatory, January 30. Available at: https://oecd.ai/en/wonk/india

Espiner, T. (2023), BT to Cut 55,000 Jobs with Upto Fifth Replaced by AI, *BBC*, May 18. Available at: https://www.bbc.com/news/business-65631168

Fleischer, V. (2010), Regulatory Arbitrage (1–52), *Texas Law Review*, 89(2).

Garcia, K. (2019), Copyright Arbitrage (199–266), *California Law Review*, 107.

Greisbach, K., Reich, A.., Elliot-Negri, M. & Milkman, R. (2019), Algorithmic Control in Platform Food Delivery Work (1–15), *Socius*, 5.

Hemrajani, N. (2018), The Jobs in India That Attract Thousands of Applicants, *BBC Worklife*, June 4. Available at: https://www.bbc.com/worklife/article/20180601-the-jobs-in-india-that-attract-millions-of-applicants

Indian Artificial Intelligence Stack (2020), AI Standardisation Committee, Department of Telecommunications, 1–44. Available at: https://www.tec.gov.in/pdf/Whatsnew/ARTIFICIAL%20INTELLIGENCE%20-%20INDIAN%20STACK.pdf

India's Booking Gig and Platform Economy: Perspectives and Recommendations on the Future of Work (2022), Available at: https://www.niti.gov.in/sites/default/files/2022-06/Policy_Brief_India%27s_Booming_Gig_and_Platform_Economy_27062022.pdf

International Consortium of Investigative Journalists (ICIJ) Available at: https://offshoreleaks.icij.org/?gclid=CjwKCAjwscGjBhAXEiwAswQqNOrney_an7rWGuJzYC3uIWVT4Z8RHc-yH9LptqaI5-jhB3r066MzsRoCY0MQAvD_BwE

Jain, G. and Parsheera, M. (2021), *Cinderella's Shoe Won't Fit Soundarya: An Audit of Facial Processing Tools on Indian Faces* (1–23). Unpub. Paper. Available at: https://arxiv.org/pdf/2112.09326.pdf

Joshi, D. (2021), The Indian Algorithmic Services: When AI Gets to Decide Who Gets Welfare, *Forbes India*, August 21. Available at: https://www.forbesindia.com/article/take-one-big-story-of-the-day/the-indian-algorithmic-services-when-ai-gets-to-decide-who-gets-welfare/69583/1

Kashyap, H. (2022), Swiggy Says Not Liable for Order's Non-Delivery by Restaurant or Delivery Partner, *Inc42*, July 16. Available at: https://inc42.com/buzz/swiggy-not-liable-orders-non-delivery-consumer-panel-inr-11000-fine/

Malhotra, A. and Puhan, B. (2022), India: Artificial Intelligence Comparative Guide, *Mondaq*. November 23. Available at: https://www.mondaq.com/india/technology/1059762/artificial-intelligence-comparative-guide

Marda, V. (2018), Artificial Intelligence Policy in India: A Framework for Engaging the Limits of Data-Driven Decision-Making (1–18), *Philosophical Transactions of the Royal Society A*, 376 (2133).

Marx, K. (n.d.), Piece Wages, in Capital Volume One. Available at: https://www.marxists.org/archive/marx/works/1867-c1/ch21.htm

Mason, S. (2018), High Pay, Low Pay: Why the Gig Economy Loves Gamification, *The Guardian*, November 20. Available at: https://www.theguardian.com/business/2018/nov/20/high-score-low-pay-gamification-lyft-uber-drivers-ride-hailing-gig-economy

Meaker, M. (2022), Australia's Standoff Against Google and Facebook Worked – Sort Of, *The Wired*, February 2. Available at: https://www.wired.co.uk/article/australia-media-code-facebook-google

Menghani, T. (2022), The Swiggy Story: How Swiggy Became India's Largest Food Delivery Platform, *The Marcom Avenue*, N.S. Available at: https://www.themarcomavenue.com/blog/the-swiggy-story-how-swiggy-became-indias-largest-food-delivery-platform/

Murgia, M. (2022), India Deploys Facial Recognition Surveilling Millions of Commuters, *Financial Times*, August 27. Available at: https://www.ft.com/content/b5e3fdc9-2fed-45f1-beff-2944da89f6c1

Naraharisetty, R. (2021), In the Gig Economy Customers Are Complicit in Labour Exploitation, *The Swaddle*, August 20. Available at: https://theswaddle.com/swiggy-zomato-labor-exploitation/

National Strategy for Artificial Intelligence:AIforAll (2018:1–114), *NitiAayog*. Available at: https://niti.gov.in/sites/default/files/2019-01/NationalStrategy-for-AI-Discussion-Paper.pdf

OECD. AI Policy Observatory: Policies for India. Available at: https://oecd.ai/en/dashboards/policy-initiatives?conceptUris=http:%2F%2Fkim.oecd.org%2FTaxonomy%2FGeographicalAreas%23India

OECD releases Pillar Two model rules for domestic implementation of 15% global minimum tax (2021), OECD, December 20. Available at: https://www.oecd.org/tax/beps/oecd-releases-pillar-two-model-rules-for-domestic-implementation-of-15-percent-global-minimum-tax.htm

Parwez, S. (2022), Covid-19 Pandemic and Work Precarity at Digital Food Platforms: A Delivery Worker's Perspective (1–10), *Social Sciences & Humanities Open*, 5.

Perappadan, B. S. (2023), CoWIN Vaccination Data Out, Centre Denies Breach, *The Hindu*, June 12. Available at: https://www.thehindu.com/news/national/health-ministry-responds-to-massive-cowin-data-breach/article66960250.ece

Pollman, E. (2019), Tech, Regulatory Arbitrage, and Limits (1–41), European Corporate Governance Institute (ECGI), Law Working Paper No. 455/2019, June. Available at: https://www.ecgi.global/sites/default/files/working_papers/documents/finalpollman.pdf

Post-grads among 35K applicants for one-year job to cut grass and catch snakes in Bengal (2023), *The New Indian Express*, June 1. Available at: https://www.newindianexpress.com/nation/2023/may/31/post-grads-among-35k-applicants-for-one-year-job-to-cut-grass-and-catch-snakes-in-bengal-2580453.html

Pritchett, L. (2023), People over Robots, *Foreign Affairs* 102(2). Available at: https://web-s-ebscohost-com.ezproxy.library.uq.edu.au/ehost/detail/detail?vid=3&sid=78cade44-24cf-447a-87f3-dcdf6150c684%40redis&bdata=JnNpdGU9ZWhvc3QtbGl2ZQ%3d%3d#AN=162037851&db=bth

Rani, Uma, Gobel, Nora, and Dhir, Rishabh Kumar (2022), Is Flexibility and Autonomy a Myth or Reality On Taxi Platforms? Comparison between Traditional and App-based Taxi Drivers in Developing Countries (167–192), in De Stefano, Valerio, Durri, Ilda, Stylogiannis, Charalampos, and Wouters, Mathias (Ed.), *A Research Agenda for the Gig Economy and Society*, Edward Elgar Publishing, Cheltenham.

Responsible AI #AIforall: Adopting the framework: A use case approach on facial recognition technology (n.d.), (1–86) *Niti Aayog*, November. Available at: https://www.niti.gov.in/sites/default/files/2022-11/Ai_for_All_2022_02112022_0.pdf

"Responsible AI for All: Adopting the Framework – A use case approach on Facial Recognition Technology" (2022:1–86), *Niti Aayog*, November. Available at: https://www.medianama.com/wp-content/uploads/2022/11/Ai_for_AII_2022_02112022-1.pdf

Safak, C. and Farrar, J. (2021), Managed by Bots: Data Driven Exploitation in the Gig Economy (1–82), *Worker Exchange Information*. Available at: https://5b88ae42-7f11-4060-85ff-4724bbfed648.usrfiles.com/ugd/5b88ae_8d720d54443543e2a928267d354acd90.pdf

Sanzgiri, V. (2022), Swiggy Collaborates with IIT Jodhpur for 'State-of-the Art Facial Recognition Technology, *Medianama*, November 16. Available at: https://www.medianama.com/2022/11/223-swiggy-iit-jodhpur-collaboration-facial-recognition/

Sarasvati. N. T. (2023), Indian Govt Says No Central Storage of Digi Yatra Data, Accountability for User Privacy Still a Question, *Medianaama*, March 17. Available at: https://www.medianama.com/2023/03/223-digi-yatra-civil-aviation-ministry-data-storage-rti/

Scheiber, N. (2017), How Uber Uses Psychological Tricks to Push Its Drivers' Buttons, *New York Times*, April 2. Available at: https://www.nytimes.com/interactive/2017/04/02/technology/uber-drivers-psychological-tricks.html

SFLC. In's Comments on the NITI Aayog Discussion Paper: Responsible AI for All: Use-Case Approach on Facial Recognition Technology (2022:1–6) Software Freedom Legal Centre, New Delhi. Available at: https://www.medianama.com/wp-content/uploads/2022/12/SFLC-comments-on-FRT-paper-by-NITI-Aayog_Nov-2022.pdf

Sharma, N. (2021), India's Delivery Workers Are Driving a Conversation about Long Hours and Low Pay, *Quartz*, September 17. Available at: https://qz.com/india/2051605/indias-gig-workers-use-social-media-to-lobby-for-better-work

Singh, M. (2020), Indian Startups Explore Alliance and Alternative App Store to Fight Google's 'Monopoly', *TechCrunch*, October 1. Available at: https://techcrunch.com/2020/09/30/indian-startups-explore-forming-an-alliance-and-alternative-app-store-to-fight-googles-monopoly/

Singh, M. (2023), India Opts Against AI Regulation, *TechCrunch*, April 6. Available at: https://techcrunch.com/2023/04/05/india-opts-against-ai-regulation/

Sivasubramaniam, A. (2021) Algorithms in India: Key Findings and Recommendations (1–22), Centre for Policy Research, State Capacity Initiative Working Paper No. 2021-1 New Delhi. Available at: https://www.cprindia.org/system/tdf/working_papers/Working%20paper_Regulating%20Algorithms_2%20Sep._re%2005.pdf?file=1&type=node&id=10022&force=1

Swiggy: Terms & Conditions. Available at: https://www.swiggy.com/terms-and-conditions

Tandon, R. & Rathi, A. (2022), Sustaining Urban Labour Markets: Situating Migration and Domestic Work in India's 'Gig' Economy (1–17), *Economy and Space*. DOI: 10.1177/0308518X221120822

Thathoo, C. (2022), Niti Aayog Proposed Data Protection Norms for Facial Recognition Technology in India, *Inc42*, November 22. Available at: https://inc42.com/buzz/niti-aayog-proposes-data-protection-norms-for-facial-recognition-technology-in-india/

The Digital Personal Data Protection Act (2023), Available at: https://www.meity.gov.in/writereaddata/files/Digital%20Personal%20Data%20Protection%20Act%202023.pdf

Vasudevan, K. and Chan, N. K. (2020), Gamification and Work Games: Examining Consent and Resistance among Uber Drivers (8660886), *New Media & Society*, 24(4).

Woodcock, J. (2020), The Algorithmic Panopticon at Deliveroo: Measurement, Precarity and the Illusion of Control (67–95), *Ephemera: Theory and Politics in Organisation*, 20 (3).

Other Resources

Manji, S. (n.d.) How Swiggy Used Data Science to Conduct Compliance Checks with the Delivery Partners, *Career Labs*. Available at: https://www.youtube.com/watch?v=INU555Uo1pE

5 Resistance

Global Resistance

The 60 million workers in the USA who were involved in one form or another of freelance work in 2021 are a fraction of the growing number of workers in the global gig economy (Wiessner, et al.: 2022) who are themselves a part of the two billion strong workforce in the informal economy (ILO:2018). Guy Standing (2011), borrowing from French social theory, has described them as the *precariat*, a new class of workers who lack the hard-won securities that traditional workers had, and who are for the most legally absent as a class of workers. The precariat includes many types of workers including those in the informal economy, casualised labour, for example, in the university systems in the West and platform workers whose work is intermediated by platforms and apps. There are two types of digital labour platforms – online web-based platforms and workers involved in a great variety of freelance work as translators, editors, designers, software programmers, etc and location-based platforms such as gig workers involved in taxi, delivery and home services (See ILO:2021). While these platforms have celebrated the flexibility and freedoms associated with gig work, gig workers, for the most part, belong to a captive workforce who are involved in casual labour and piecemeal work in what until recently has been an unregulated environment. Pant and Majumder (2022:86), call it the 'new employment model' and argue that it gives workers autonomy, flexibility and opportunities for women while giving platforms opportunities to hire freelancers, with fewer obligations on their part as employers to their 'partners' and access to talent on demand. While they do point out some of the challenges faced by gig workers, this new employment situation is largely seen as a win-win situation for both the partner and the platform. The lack of regulatory oversight and consistent misclassification of the gig labour force has enabled the key gig platforms across the ride-hail (Uber, Lyft and Ola), food delivery (Deliveroo, Swiggy and Zomato) and homework (TaskRabbit) sectors to algorithmically manage worker earnings for piecework and treat their employees as contractual staff who are not entitled to benefits, including pensions, vacation and health insurance. Snider (2018:564) has observed that in the US gig economy '....employers are legally enabled to evade virtually every

DOI: 10.4324/9781003491705-6

benefit attained by workers over the last 100 plus years of struggle', a stance aided by the fact that the US Fair Labour Standards did not apply to the so-called '1099' workers (derived from Internal Revenue Service's Form 1099 to be completed by contract workers, freelancers) 'who are not classified as employees' (568). The Biden administration has attempted to overturn the Trump-era Independent Contractor Status Under the Fair Labor Standards Act (2021 IC Rule) with a revised rule that reduces the risk of worker misclassification and enables the security and rights of gig workers (See US Dept of Labor & Ivanova:2022). This contestation at a federal level is a reflection of battles fought at a state level in a number of states in the USA including most famously in California where a pro-Gig worker Bill (AB5:2019) that placed the onus on platform intermediaries to pass an 'ABC' test to classify workers as contractors was contested by Proposition 22 in 2020 after a $200 million lobbying effort by Uber, Lyft and other platform companies. 'California's Prop 22 was a ballot initiative led by app-based companies such as Uber, Lyft, and DoorDash to exclude ride-hail and food-delivery app-based workers from nearly all employee rights under state law, including the right to a minimum wage, time-and-a-half for overtime, expenses reimbursement, and benefits such as unemployment compensation and state workers' compensation'(Chen & Padin:2021). Prop 22 has since been deemed unconstitutional and struck down by the Alameda Superior Court, California (See Romeo:2021).

The Case of Glovo

The Directives of the European Parliament and of the Council on improving working conditions in platform work, Brussels (2021) highlights the fact that 28 million workers in the EU were employed as gig workers in 2021, a figure projected to rise to 43 million in 2025. While the EC has been involved in creating enabling legislation supportive of the interests of gig workers, there have been variations in how individual states have responded to the need to regulate this sector. While Germany has consistently supported the interests of traditional taxi drivers and resisted the 'Uberisation' of this sector, France and the UK have seen major contestations between worker unions and platform companies, other countries such as Spain have been involved in creating a legal environment supportive of the interests of gig workers. Spain's Rider's Law, 11 May 2021 forces the platform to divulge the specific nature of algorithmic management used by the platform to manage their 'workers' and includes the presumption that platform workers in the food delivery business are in a dependent relation with their employers. In September 2022, the Supreme Court provided the following legal reasons for why the food delivery platform Glovo's workers should be considered employees:

- Platform workers work under Glovo's trademark;
- The essential means of production in the activity are not the platform worker's cell phone or motorcycle, but the digital platform itself;

- The rating mechanism acts as a form of surveillance and control of the platform workforce, thereby limiting platform workers' freedom of choice regarding work schedules;
- Glovo does not as a mere intermediary but as a delivery company;
- Glovo makes all the commercial decisions of the business;
- The price, the method of payment and remuneration is fixed exclusively by Glovo;
- The platform worker had no involvement in the negotiations between Glovo and the companies whose products are delivered, nor in the relationship between Glovo and the customers to whom the orders are delivered.

(Spain: The Rider's Law....2)

Rather than comply with this legislation, Deliveroo decided to wind up its business in Spain resulting in the loss of 3000 jobs and Glovo, citing the Rider's Law 'presumption' of employment, decided to terminate 10,000 of its workers and retain 2000 on contracts (See Aranguez:2021). Glovo has been regularly fined by Spanish courts for continuing to frame evasive classifications of their workers as 'autonomous' including in 2022 when they were fined $78 million for classifying 10,614 workers as self-employed in Barcelona and Valencia when it was argued that the workers were in an employment relationship with the company (Lomas:2022). Glovo's tactics are by no means uncommon. On 8 June 2023, the GMB Union that was trying for recognition at Amazon's Coventry warehouse withdrew its bid after securing the needed numbers (800) after Amazon recruited 1000 extra staff to scupper the bid (Espiner & Conway:2023).

The Multifaceted Nature of Worker Resistance

Worker resistance to these platforms has taken the following forms:

1 Legal resistance has been launched in different jurisdictions around the world, for instance, by the European Commission and the Federal Trade Commission in the USA (See FTC Policy Statement:2022) with varying levels of impact. Typically, these platforms have been involved in counter-litigation. For example, Proposition 22 in California, consistently contested the use of words and terms that would give workers rights, employed lobbyists and stalled the journey of draft legislation from becoming legally binding.
2 The involvement of both established and platform worker–specific unions in bargaining and negotiating for worker's rights. These too are at a nascent stage of development. The increasing number of workers in the gig economy has led to belated efforts by established unions to fight for their cause (See Page-Tickell & Ritchie:2020).

3 NGOs such as Fairwork located at the Oxford Internet Institute that is involved in rating platforms across the world. Foundations such as the Ford Foundation, the Open Society Foundation and Mercy Corps. State-based initiatives such as the Gig Economy Initiative in Germany (See BMZ, Digital Global).
4 State support for platform alternatives. For example, Kerala Savaari is an e-taxi service that was launched by the Government of Kerala's Kerala Motor Transport Worker's Welfare Fund Board in August 2022. The scheme involves state subsidisation of fuel- and insurance-related costs, fixed rates and no price surges (The News Minute: 2022). In direct contrast with the tendency in India to marginalise public telecommunication entities, the 'Palakkad wing of Indian Telephone Industries (ITI) Limited, a public sector undertaking under the Union government, is in charge of GPS facility, application software and call centre operations' (Prince:2021).
5 Everyday resistance involving gig workers who are involved in tactical resistance that includes non-compliance, evasion of algorithmic management and worker solidarities expressed through shared apps (See Vasudevan & Keung Chan: 2022, Mosseri:2022, Hao & Freischland:2022, Cini:2023, Anwar & Graham:2022, Cant:2019). In terms of research, this type of resistance offers opportunities to investigate the great many 'hidden transcripts' used by workers in the gig economy to contest, bypass, subvert and reinforce agency in the context of an 'at a distance' relationship with platforms. Mustika and Savirani (2021:56–57) in an article on the everyday resistance of motorcycle taxi drivers in Yogyakarta highlight the fact that they use both technological (ghost accounts) and non-technological means 'Drivers label modified or hacked versions of the official Gojek application as *akun tuyal*, a term that translates as 'ghost accounts' and is also used to refer to the making of "fictive orders" (*order fiktif*). Such modified applications are not available through the Google Play store but links are circulated amongst drivers through various channels, including social media platforms like Telegram and Facebook'.

Resistance in India

Resistance in India needs to be seen in a context in which the employment generated by the platform economy is seen as a wholly positive development by the GoI. This is highlighted in a report produced by NITI Aayog (2022), India's Booming Gig and Platform Economy that estimates a gig economy workforce of 24 million people in 2029 from the close to 8 million employed in this sector in 2020(3) (See Nair:2019). This report celebrates the fact that women and people with disabilities will benefit from this economy, although their welfare will depend on better work conditions, benefits and job security that this sector lacks. However, this report glosses over the fact that workers in the gig economy really are an extension of workers in the unorganised sector

– a reality that does not call for any celebration. Punia (2020) in an article on workers in the unorganised sector in India highlights the fact that 90 per cent of the workforce (451 million in 2018) consists of informal workers. The fact that nine out of ten workers in India are in the informal economy stands as an inditement of a system that has not been able to expand access to work in the formal economy (Jadhav:2022). Mehrotra (2019:1) in an ILO working paper on the informal economy in India highlights a sobering fact '.....with over 90 per cent of the entire workface being informal (defined as those without any social insurance), and 85 per cent of the non-agricultural workforce being informal, India is an outlier among low-middle income countries in this regard. Although India is one of the fastest growing large economies in the world, the informality incidence has remained stuck at this level for decades'. It is in this context of precarity that one needs to evaluate India's economic successes, successes that are sector-specific and that are arguably only of benefit to a small group of people. While India Stack's success as a national project does highlight the country's prowess in the implementation of large-scale tech projects, its beneficiaries on the whole consist mainly of the precariat that includes gig workers. Slavok Zizek (2009:37–38) in his volume *First as Tragedy, Then as Farce* and the RSA animated version of this text critiques the compassionate core at the heart of cultural capitalism. Zizek argues that the integration of compassion into acts of consumption – such as drinking a cup of fair-trade sourced coffee at Starbucks enables consumers to experience a 'coffee karma' but that makes invisible the need to address the real issues behind fair-trade coffee. The compassion that slave owners had for their slaves kept slaves from revolting. Charity is the worst form of exploitation because it deals with the symptoms and not with the causes. If one were to be cynical of India Stack, its efficiencies make invisible the reality of precarity. I am not for a moment arguing against the need for welfare as it does play an extraordinarily important role in helping people survive. I am arguing that welfare does not address the causes of poverty or for that matter unemployment.

While there is certainly evidence of nationwide organising and unionising of gig workers in India, the understanding of 'resistance' needs to be nuanced precisely because very typically, gig workers often like the flexibility associated with work in a context in which access to employment remains a major issue. The extent of the informal economy in India suggests that there are bound to be many complicities with informality, many opportunities for entrepreneurism in the contexts of informality and a multiplicity of opportunities for informal work in a working day. Domestics who work in India typically work in a couple of houses and may work afterhours doing piecemeal work. The gig work economy attracts both those for whom work is the only income and those for whom gig work is a source of secondary income or an opportunity to earn for students, professionals and others from the working classes. Taken in this sense, resistance will be stronger among those for whom working with Swiggy or Uber in India is their full-time occupation as opposed to those who are involved in multiple forms of gig work. Given the precarity of work and the always-present danger of algorithmic redundancy, most platform workers will be cautious of taking part in strike actions and demonstrations that may leave them exposed to the whims of algorithmic management. Soriano and Cabanes (2020:9), in an article on the entrepreneurial solidarities of gig workers in Facebook groups in the Philippines, highlight the precarity, ambiguity and opportunities that exist for gig workers in an economy that extolls the virtues of and earning capacities from gig work. Facebook acts as a site for the reconciliation of contradictions and as a space to explore entrepreneurial opportunities although, as Soriano and Cabanes, observe 'the entrepreneurial solidarities that emerge from the Facebook groups also serve to dampen possibilities to meaningfully challenge the structures of power underlying digital platform labour….In sum, Facebook groups serve as spaces for the articulation of discontent and sharing strategies for coping and success, but also generate 'entrepreneurial solidarities' rather than enacting substantial pressure upon platforms to address oppressive conditions'. Anwar and Graham (2019) on gig worker relationships with the remote task platform Upwork in Africa make a similar point to Soriano and Cabanes on the graded nature of resistance and differences in resistance between new and old workers, the experienced and the inexperienced and those who have learned how to negotiate wages, rate difficult clients and game platforms in their favour. As remote task workers, work is individual and therefore the chances for unionising are limited. Hence, resistance is an individual response to the need for agency. Gig workers depending on the type of work they are involved in are involved in either individual or collective acts of resistance. Wood and Lehdonvirta (2021) in an article on gig work in North America, the UK and the Philippines have argued the case for what they term the 'subordinated agency' of gig workers who experience agency towards clients through choosing 'clients, rates, tasks and methods and times of working' (1398) and subordination towards platforms that they are dependent on and which they are involved as subordinates (1390). I am of the opinion that in the case of India and its hierarchies, agency is exercised by some platform workers such as Ola/Uber drivers (although they too are dependent on client ratings and reviews) but certainly not by food delivery workers who are, in terms of education and social and political capital, in the marginal position of being a part of the vulnerable precariat. Rachmawati, et aI (2021) in an article on 'ojek' riders in Indonesia observe that these riders have little agency either with clients or with the platforms. I will, in this chapter focus on collective resistance in India as a form of contentious politics in line with the work of social movement theorist Charles Tilly primarily because there is clarity with respect to the objectives of collective bargaining. The Indian case of gig worker resistance does not stand alone but relates to global initiatives that are aimed at strengthening worker conditions, salaries and benefits while also making algorithmic management accountable. The success of such initiatives can impact the lives of task-based, home-based online gig workers – particularly in areas such as monitoring and surveillance. While micro-resistance offers textured insights into the contextual nature of resistance, it does not contribute to the understanding of transformative change in the lives of gig workers. While Mona Lilja (2022:316) in her theorisation of resistance makes a case for three types of resistance formations – 'reverse discourse, spatial resistance and networked dissent' along with discursive resistance, the application of these concepts to the understanding of gig workers is unclear since the objective of resistance is primarily directed towards the creation of better working conditions, wages and management that is based on transparency. While I do acknowledge the need for a variety of enactments of resistance, I am of the view that resistance outcomes differ in their quality to engender real, material change in the lives of workers. There is the added complexity that micro-resistance might well consist of acts that contribute to the mere survival of gig workers and to outcomes that are transitory and unrelated to sustainable social change. Since remote workers' skills and platform reputation are paramount, wages often differ for the same task, there are opportunities to undercut and create micro-monopolies over very specific, specialised tasks thus limiting competition. Wood et al. (2019:70) have observed that apart from a narrow subsection of workers who use their skill and reputational capital to earn high incomes, for the majority 'The autonomy resulting from algorithmic control can lead to overwork, sleep deprivation and exhaustion as a consequence of the weak structural power of workers vis-a-vis clients'.

Gender and Resistance

One of the more egregious examples of digital labour platforms exploiting workers is the case of the online beauty and home services platform – Urban Company ($2.8 bn valuation). It is often the case that gig worker resistance in the ride share and delivery industries is often spearheaded by male gig workers. This is because only a small percentage of these workers are women. In online beauty services, however, the majority of workers are women. In October 2021, a number of beauticians and spa attendants who worked for Urban Company went on strike against low wages, high commissions and poor working conditions including the lack of toilets, a perennial issue faced by women workers in India across all working sectors. Worker protests were also directed against the expectation that well-performing workers (Luxe/Gold Plus & Silver Plus) were asked to provide a ten per cent discount to customers thus negating their own strong work ethic and commitment to the company through the delivery of services (Gauri Lankesh News Desk:2021). While the company did respond by announcing a 12-point agenda that included transparency and better wages, it also included a new flexi category for workers who opted out of a new subscription-scheme based on an upfront fee. When these gig workers protested against these new schemes, Urban Company sued these workers and 'sought a permanent prohibitory injunction from the court restraining the women from holding any 'demonstration, dharna, rally, gherao, peace march, shouting slogans, entering or assembling on or near the office premises"' in Gurugram, New Delhi (See Ara:2021). The lawsuit reiterated typical platform exceptionalism and stated that the 'company is only an aggregator' connecting customers to service professionals who are 'independent workers' that 'voluntarily work' and are 'free to decide when and where they wish to work'. It argues that a 'certain group of disruptive Partners...have decided to repeatedly derail the collaborative and cooperative process for their unknown ulterior motives and vested interests' (Mehrotra:2022). While the civil judge involved in the matter found the company's argument 'devoid of merits' following which the company withdrew its suit, it sought to block accounts of those involved in the strike actions and used the excuse of poor performance to deny those involved work (Lakshman:2022). Dhar and Thuppilikkat (2022:683) in an article on this struggle highlight both the strength of women organisers and their use of WhatsApp for mobilising, networking, engendering solidarities and networking with traditional trade unions the weakness of what they term 'informal unionism' that includes their unsystematic approach to raising funds, weak organisational efficiency and lack of defined roles and leadership.

FinTech for Gig Workers

Quite fundamentally, resistance by gig workers in India is a response to a State that is ideologically committed to celebrating India's success stories while ignoring the reality of growing disparities and uneven development. The gig economy is part of the latter story. The institutions and agencies that make up the GoI are involved in the manufacture of feel-good stories of India's ascendence as a world power, its achievements in science and technology, financial inclusion, poverty alleviation and reaching its employment targets that are in turn, faithfully reproduced by dominant media that quite uncritically communicate this narrative. It is quite extraordinary that there are now FinTech companies such as the subscription-based KarmaLife that specifically cater to the financial needs of platform workers by facilitating loans via loan strategies in partnership with data aggregators. While credit lines from traditional sources such as banks are difficult for workers in the unorganised sector to access, these new FinTech companies really do function as digital moneylenders to the most vulnerable in society. KarmaLife's app enables auto repayment of loans from worker payouts although loans are based on the monitoring of worker accounts, behaviours, payment histories and ratings. Their official tagline is that they are 'Empowering India's Workforce'! KarmaLife offers Earned Wage Access (EWA) — a financial product that gives people access to a portion of their salaries any time before payday; this is essentially like a small credit in the present, that is based on future earnings. This reduces the risk KarmaLife takes on its books, while also being able to provide its users access to quick loans (Saxena:2022). Another FinTech company, Refyne also caters to the working class and offers a salary-on-demand and salary top-up services that basically give workers an equivalent salary or adds to it before it is due at the end of the month. Their privacy policy is unequivocal about monitoring and collecting user data.

- Refyne may use cookies to monitor and manage your usage of the Refyne platform including, without limitation, for simplifying your experience when you return to Refyne platform, like remembering your login ID and certain Personal Information, deliver relevant content based on your preferences, usage patterns and location, tracking etc.
- Refyne may collect details about your use of the Refyne platform and/or Products and Service, such as the features used, any activity carried out and the frequency/duration/time thereof the actions taken etc.
- Refyne may access, use and collect organisational contact data of the user from their hand-held device to empower users to share the app with their co-workers and promote financial wellness at work.

(Refyne:Privacy Policy)

Gig Workers and the Law

Official statistics has been compromised and think tanks such as NITI Aayog churn out gushing reports on India's economic development and projections for even stronger growth in the years to come. NITI Aayog's (2022) report, *India's Booming Gig and Platform Economy: Perspectives and recommendations on the future of work*, is an example of a collective mindset that projects progress for women and people with disabilities in the gig economy but whose recommendations are only haltingly, selectively operationalised, if at all. This is highlighted in the fact that out of the four labour laws that were enacted in 2020 – the Code on Wages, 2019, the Industrial Relations Code, 2020, the Code on Social Security, 2020 and the Occupational Safety, Health and Working Conditions Code, 2020, only the Code on Social Security explicitly addresses the need for social security cover for workers in the unorganised sectors, gig and platform economies. However, these recommendations are yet to be enacted since the expenses to cover social security are to be shared between the private sector and the central and state governments and that are still being negotiated. The Indian Federation of App-based Transport Workers (IFAT) has submitted a Public Interest Litigation (PIL) to the Supreme Court that argues that in lieu of the non-enforcement of the social security code gig workers should be allowed access to benefits outlined in the Unorganised Worker's Social Security Act, 2008 (See Shroff:2021). The code highlights the fact that for workers to avail themselves of benefit entitlements, they will need to register their Aadhar identification card on the Shram Suvidha labour portal – 'Under the Code, every unorganised worker, gig worker or platform worker who has completed 16 (sixteen) years of age has to be registered, with Aadhar, on self-declaration basis in the form on the Shram Suvidha Portal. Provided that such worker has been engaged as gig worker or platform worker, for not less than 90 (ninety) days during the preceding 12 (twelve) months. Further, the Central Government will be formulating suitable welfare schemes for gig workers and platform workers on matters pertaining to life and disability cover, accident insurance, health and maternity benefits, old age protection, creche, etc' (The Legal500:2023). It is unclear if they will also have to register on the e-Shram portal, a National Database of Unorganised Workers established by the Ministry of Labour and Employment. This excessive emphasis on digital enrolment as the basis for entitlements apart from increasing the surveillance of platform workers who have already been objectified by the apps that they use can negatively impact those workers in the informal sector, for example, workers belonging to indigenous communities who have not enrolled on Aadhar or those whose biometrics have consistently failed the authentication test. The code expects aggregators to contribute between 1 and 2 per cent of their annual turnover to this fund. Aggregators are also expected to register gig workers and provide regular data on the gig workers employed by them (Mahanta & Saha:2023).

Gig Workers and Unions

It is in the context of this impasse that traditional forms of resistance by gig workers including demonstrations and strikes have become widespread along with attempts to organise and unionise gig workers – both stand-alone unions such as the Ola–Uber Drivers and Owner's Association (OUDOA), the Telangana Gig and Platform worker's Union (TGPWU), the Indian Federation of App-based Transport Workers (IFAT), Sarvodaya Driver's Association of Delhi, the App Cab Driver's Union (Kolkata), Tamilnadu Food and Other Products Delivery Worker's Union, Online Workers Delivery Union, Kerala and unions associated with the more established unions in India such as the All India Gig Worker's Union (AIGWU) that is associated with the Centre for Indian Trade Unions (CITU) associated with the Communist Party of India (Marxist), the United Food Delivery Partner's Union linked to the Socialist Unity Centre of India and The West Bengal Online Cab Operator's Guild linked to the Trinamool Congress (See Dhar:2022). Between 2016 and 2018, there have been 15 major Ola–Uber driver–related strikes in India along with strikes by food delivery partners linked to Uber-Eats, Swiggy and Zomato in Tier-1–3 cities across India. These strikes have forced governments to mediate and given the potential of these workers as vote-banks, enabled small victories such as the Chief Minister of Maharashtra putting forward the idea for the need for a single cab-aggregator app in Mumbai making markets and pricing more transparent. These strikes have also led to new alliances between other service workers such as nurses and forced established trade unions to take cognisance of the needs of platform and gig workers. In one of the better articles on resistance by gig workers in India, Aditya Ray (2019) writes of the new challenges that established unions face in the context of contentious actions by gig and platform workers and the steady increase in gig worker demands taken seriously by established political parties.

'In Mumbai, a city with a longer history of labour organisation and strikes, Ola and Uber drivers pulled support from traditional unions with mass membership bases in the city. This was clear as the strike action of March 2017 that came to be led by the *Marathi Kamgar Sena* (MKS), a union affiliated to the right-wing *Maharashtra Navnirman Sena* (MNS). Whereas, another strike action lasting several days, over October and November 2018, was fronted by representatives from the *Maharashtra Rashtriya Rajya Kamgar Sangh* (MRRKS), the union associated with the centrist National Congress Party (NCP), which boasts large presence among urban and rural middle classes as well as backward social caste groups. Some of the local politicians of the Indian National Congress (INC), the main opposition party at the centre, were also seen speaking vocally on the issue of drivers' rights'. A major development in support of gig workers' rights is the move by the government of Rajasthan to establish a Gig Worker's Welfare Act based on a 200-crore allocation during the 2023–2024 budget on 11 February 2023 although it needs to be operationalised (Sanzgiri:2023).

Making Sense of Resistance

A special section of the *International Journal of Communications* 2023 (17) is dedicated to the understanding of Worker Resistance in Digital Capitalism and includes case studies from the Philippines and Indonesia and chapters on both formal and everyday resistance. There is a welcoming optimism after what has been close to two decades of gig worker exploitation aided by the politics of regulatory arbitrage. However, as opposed to academic studies that rather typically focus on the subversion of algorithms, tactical resistance and cultural struggle, an ILO (2022) report that is based on data drawn from the Leeds Index of Platform Labour Protest includes findings from 1,271 worker protests from around the world. The study includes data from protests in four sectors – 'ride-hailing, food delivery, courier services and grocery delivery' (5). While the methods of protest and repertoires of contention include 'critical mass' rideouts, where large numbers of cyclists ride slowly around a city centre, slowing traffic; flash mobs, where groups of workers appear suddenly at a venue such as a company headquarters and conduct a brief, noisy and disruptive protest; street rallies involving workers and supporters; publicity stunts and the widespread use of colour and sound, in the form of flags, flares and sound systems (9), traditional demonstrations are the most common means of protest in support of traditional issues linked to unions – in particular, pay rise, followed by employment status and health and safety. The study concludes on a cautionary note. There is a need to factor in the centrality of basic issues such as pay rather than overemphasise novel forms of cultural resistance that do exist but are limited in terms of what they can achieve over the long term. 'Our findings suggest both notable similarities and differences among platform worker protests across the world. The analysis shows that pay is universally a pre-eminent concern for platform workers and tends to be the subject of protests in all regions of the world. Indeed, the overwhelming presence of pay as the major cause of platform worker protest suggests that we need to be cautious about centralizing issues such as algorithmic control. Moreover, while much scholarship places emphasis on forms of online activity such as the subversion of algorithms, our findings show that more traditional methods, such as strikes and demonstrations, are also widely used in platform worker protests' (32).

A global analysis of worker protest in digital labour platforms In India, though lacking the legal recognition of gig workers, has been a fundamental issue and typically the government veers towards vendors representing their workers. Since their work hours are typically extensive, they are not covered under the Minimum Wages Act (1948), cannot be paid overtime and do not have the benefit of a pension/provident fund. They are also not recognised as an 'employee' and as such even the unions that represent them, do not have, as yet the recognition that other, established trade unions have. Gig workers do not have the right to make their case in a labour court but only in civil or criminal courts (Duggal:2023).

The State Resisting Big Tech: Coops and The Kerala Story

Resistance comes in many forms. It is unusual for resistance to be shaped and nurtured by individual states in India, although their contributions simply need to be factored into a larger understanding of resistance such as state support for the Bengaluru Auto Rickshaws Drivers' Union launch of the Namma Yatri app that was specifically a response to the anti-competitive practice of the Ola/Uber duopoly. The proposed Rajasthan Platform-Based Gig Workers Social Security and Welfare Fund that will be funded from seed funds as well as a minimal tax on the money paid for a consumer to the aggregator is the first of its kind in India (Saini: 2023). This fund is a political statement in the absence of the GoI's implementation of its Code of Social Security (2020) and its provision for a Social Security Fund for the welfare of platform and gig workers. The state that has invested the most in people-friendly platforms supportive of the rights of workers is the Southern Indian state of Kerala. They have launched two ride-sharing platform cooperatives – Yatri, a taxi drivers' platform cooperative and Auto Savaari, an auto-hailing app by an auto cooperative (Sasidharan & Krishnan: 2023) that is a reflection of an ambitious attempt to establish 4000 platform cooperatives based on a community ownership model. Platform cooperatives' tenets strike a balance between the access economy (peer-to-peer sharing), the community-based economy (an economic system that promotes local exchange) and the platform economy (Dave:2022). Yatri had a 4.2 rating on Google Playstore. Its origins are as a coop consisting of a thousand drivers belonging to five trade unions linked to the Kerala Metropolitan Transport Authority (Krishnakumar, Korjan & bp admin:2021). The government also launched a food delivery app Rezoy that is owned by the Kerala Hotel and Restaurant Association, an apex body whose membership is 40,000 strong – an association that took the decision to not cooperate with the dominant app-based delivery companies including Swiggy and Zomato. The government of Kerala has a Department of Cooperation under which there are 16,256 coops in agricultural credit, PDS, health, education, housing and women's development among other areas (Dept. of Coop). This coop ecosystem is a natural space for platform coops. Scholz and Calzada (2021) describe the benefits of a data coop.

> The ownership of assets has profound implications on many aspects of life; it impacts income inequality and, concretely, the daily experiences in the workplace. With cooperative ownership, members jointly decide the rules of the game. Responsibly collecting, storing, and sharing data is key to unlocking its potential. Governance of such data means that the data rights of communities are protected, and the use of data is fair and focused on social benefit. It changes the current paradigm of individuals surrendering data to large tech companies to a community ownership system. Communities retain data rights, accountability, legal standards, and fiduciary representation. With data coops, data collection focuses on what is beneficial for communities. They decide which data are collected about them and for what purpose.

Kerala's engagement with these digital platforms is yet to be evaluated. There are reports on the fact that the Kerala Knowledge Economy Mission's (KKEM) projects aimed at closing the unemployment gap have not been successful, particularly for women who lag behind in terms of employment, a critique of AI-related processes, and the fact that the Digital Workforce Management System – the technical layer – collects personal data leading to uncertainty about how this data is used in the absence of privacy laws (Sapni:2021). While such critiques are necessary, it would be important to point out that in the present political dispensation in India, Kerala's Communist government and its historical successes in subduing Big Tech including its support for FOSS (Free and Open Source Software), public sector software and now the dominant platforms and its support for a variety of citizen-based initiatives such as coops and the women's empowerment project Kudambashree are seen as anti-capitalist by the centralising government in power and the corporate sector who have traditionally resisted social initiatives implemented by this Communist Party–run state. The Reserve Bank of India's attempts to restrict coop banking in Kerala (Babu:2021) are typical of attempts to curb the exercise of federalist power by individual state governments in India, especially those that are ruled by regional parties and that are in opposition to the BJP.

Bibliography

"Kerala Savari" by Kerala Government: Three Things to Know (2022), *The News Minute*, August 23. Available at: https://www.thenewsminute.com/article/kerala-savari-cab-service-kerala-government-three-things-know-167106

Anwar, M. A. and Graham, M. (2019), Hidden Transcripts of the Gig Economy: Labour Agency and the New Art of Resistance (1269–1291), *Environment & Space* 52(7).
Anwar, M. A. & Graham, M. (2022), Resilience, Reworking and Resistance: Hidden Transcripts of the Gig Economy (154–179), in Anwar, M. A. and Graham, M. *The Digital Continent: Placing Africa in Planetary Networks of Work*, Oxford University Press, Oxford.
Ara, I (2021), India: Urban Company Files Lawsuit against Women Workers Protesting Policy Changes They Allege Impact Workers' Wages, reproduced from *The Wire*, December 23 in Business & Human Rights Resource Centre. Available at: https://www.business-humanrights.org/en/latest-news/india-urban-company-files-lawsuit-against-women-workers-protesting-policy-changes-they-allege-restricts-workers-wages-freedom-2/
Aranguez, A. (2021), Platforms Put a Spoke in the Wheels of Spain's 'Riders' 'law, *Social Europe*, September 2. Available at: https://www.socialeurope.eu/platforms-put-a-spoke-in-the-wheels-of-spains-riders-law
Babu, R. (2021), Kerala Govt Protests RBI's Directives on Co-Operatives, *Hindustan Times*, December 1. Available at: https://www.hindustantimes.com/india-news/kerala-govt-protests-rbi-s-directives-on-cooperatives-101638300759957.html
Bessa, I., Joyce, S., Neuman, D., Trappman, V. and Umney, C. (2022), A Global Analysis of Work Protest in Digital Labour Platforms (1–47). ILO Working Paper 70, July. Available at: https://www.ilo.org/wcmsp5/groups/public/---dgreports/---inst/documents/publication/wcms_849215.pdf
BMZ, Digital Global, Fair Gig Work. Available at: https://www.bmz-digital.global/en/overview-of-initiatives/gig-economy/#:~:text=The%20Gig%20Economy%20Initiative%20develops,demand%20skills%20and%20their%20rights
California Assembly Bill 5. https://leginfo.legislature.ca.gov/faces/billTextClient.xhtml?bill_id=201920200AB5
Cant, C. (2019) *Riding for Deliveroo: Resistance in the New Economy*, Polity, Cambridge/Metford MA
Chen, B. & Padin, L. (2021), Prop 22 Was a Failure for California's App-Based Workers. Now It's also Unconstitutional, *National Employment Law Project*, September 16. Available at: https://www.nelp.org/blog/prop-22-unconstitutional/
Cini, L. (2023), Resisting Algorithmic Control: Understanding the Rise and Variety of Platform Worker Mobilisations (125–144), *New Technology, Work & Employment*, 38.
Dave, M. (2022), Kerala Plans to Launch 4,000 Platform Coops to Upskill Unemployed Youth, *Platform Cooperativism Consortium*, May 12. Available at: https://platform.coop/blog/kerala-plans-to-launch-4000-platform-co-ops-to-upskill-unemployed-youth/
Depart of Cooperation. Available at: https://cooperation.kerala.gov.in/2019/04/06/introduction/
Dhar, D. (2022), Organising the Unorganised: How Gig Workers in India Are Fighting Back against Low Pay and Precarious Employment, *Rose Luxemburg Stiftung*, July 8. Available at: https://www.rosalux.de/en/news/id/46886/organizing-the-unorganized-1
Dhar, D. and Thuppilikkat, A. A. (2022), Gendered Labour's Positions of Vulnerabilities in Digial Labour Platforms and Strategies of Resistance: A Case Study of Women Worker's Struggle in Urban Company, New Delhi (667–686), *Gender & Development*, 30(3).
Directive of the European Parliament and of the Council on Improving Working Conditions in Platform Work (2021), *European Commission, Brussels*, 1–44. Available at: https://eur-lex.europa.eu/legal-content/EN/TXT/PDF/?uri=CELEX:52021PC0762
Duggal, D. (2023), Why Gig Workers in India Can't Unionise, Despite Poor Working Conditions? *Moneycontrol*, May 14. Available at: https://www.moneycontrol.com/

news/trends/features/why-gig-workers-in-india-despite-poor-working-conditions-cant-unionise-10583981.html
Espiner, T. and Conway, Z. (2023), GMB Union Accuses Amazon UK of 'Dirty Tricks' in Recognition Battle, *BBC*, June 9. Available at: https://www.bbc.com/news/business-65848585
FTC Policy Statement on Gig Work (2022: 1–17), Federal Trade Commission, September 15. Available at: https://www.bmz-digital.global/wp-content/uploads/2023/02/India-Rating-2022.pdf
Hao, K. and Freischland, N. (2022), The Gig Workers Fighting Back Against Algorithms, *MIT Technology Review*, April 21. Available at: https://www.technologyreview.com/2022/04/21/1050381/the-gig-workers-fighting-back-against-the-algorithms/
India's Booming Gig and Platform Economy: Perspectives and Recommendations on the Future of Work (2022:1–16), Policy Brief, Niti Aayog. Available at: https://www.niti.gov.in/sites/default/files/2022-06/Policy_Brief_India%27s_Booming_Gig_and_Platform_Economy_27062022.pdf
Ivanova, I. (2022), Biden Administration Proposed New Rule that Could Upend "Gig" Work, *CBS News*, October 11. Available at: https://www.cbsnews.com/news/biden-administration-proposes-new-rule-that-could-make-gig-workers-full-time-employees/
Jadhav, R. (2022), Human Capital: Why Informal Employment Poses a Major Challenge for India, *The Hindu Business Line*, November 23. Available at: https://www.thehindubusinessline.com/data-stories/data-focus/why-informal-employment-poses-a-major-challenge-for-india/article66173037.ece
KarmaLife. https://www.karmalife.ai/
Krishnakumar, S., Korjan, A. and BP admin (2021), Worker-Led Alternatives: A Line of Hope for New Platform Futures, *Bot Populi*, October 21. Available at: https://botpopuli.net/worker-led-alternatives-a-line-of-hope-for-new-platform-futures/
Lakshman, A. (2022) Women Who Protested Against Urban Company Denied Jobs, *The Hindu*, June 10. Available at: https://www.thehindu.com/news/national/women-who-protested-against-urban-company-denied-jobs/article65520878.ece
Lilja, M. (2022), Theorising Resistance Formations: Reverse Discourses, Spatial Resistance and Networked Dissent (309–329), *Global Society*, 36(3).
Lomas, N. (2022), Glovo Fined $78 Million for Labour Breaches in Spain, *TechCrunch*, September 23. Available at: https://techcrunch.com/2022/09/22/glovo-labor-fine/
Mahanta, N. and Saha, S. (2023), India's New Labor Codes: Recognition of Gig and Platform Workers, *The National Law Review*, January 5. Available at: https://www.natlawreview.com/article/india-s-new-labor-codes-recognition-gig-and-platform-workers
Mehrotra, K. (2022), 'We're Being Pushed into Poverty': Voices of Women Who Took on the Unicorn Start-Up Urban Company, *Scroll.in*, January 13. Available at: https://scroll.in/magazine/1014700/were-being-pushed-into-poverty-voices-of-women-who-took-on-the-unicorn-start-up-urban-company
Mehrotra, S. (2019), Informal Employment Trends in the Indian Economy: Persistent Informality But Growing Positive Development (1–31), Employment, Working Paper No.254, Employment Policy Dept., International Labour Union. Available at: https://www.ilo.org/wcmsp5/groups/public/---ed_emp/---ifp_skills/documents/publication/wcms_734503.pdf
More than 60 per cent of the world's employed population are in the informal economy (2018), ILO Press release, April 30. Available at: https://www.ilo.org/global/about-the-ilo/newsroom/news/WCMS_627189/lang--en/index.htm
Mosseri, S. (2022), Being Watched Ad Being Seen: Negotiating Visibility in the NYC Ride-Hail Circuit (600–620), *New Media & Society* 24(3).

Mustika, A. and Savirani, A. (2021), 'Ghost Accounts', 'Joki Accounts' and 'Account Therapy': Everyday Resistance among Ride-Hailing Motorcycles Drivers in Yogyakarta, Indonesia (48–67), *The Copenhagen Journal of Asian Studies*, 39(1).
Nair, G. (2019) Can the Spirit of California's Gig Economy Bill Spread to India?, *The Wire*, September 19. Available at: https://thewire.in/business/can-the-spirit-of-californias-gig-economy-bill-spread-to-india
Notice of Proposed Rule: Employee or Independent Contractor Classification Under the Fair Labor Standards Act, RIN 1235-AA43 (2022), US Dept. of Labor, Wage and Hour Division, October 13. Available at: https://www.dol.gov/agencies/whd/flsa/misclassification/rulemaking
Page-Tickell, R. & Ritchie, J. (2020) Presence and Pretence: Trade Unions and the Gig Economy (63–87), in Page-Tickell, R. and Yerby, E. (Ed.) *Conflict and Shifting Boundaries in the Gig Economy: An Interdisciplinary Analysis* (*The Changing Context of Managing People*), Emerald Publishing Limited, Bingley.
Pant, J. J. & Majumder, M. G. (2022), Themes and Narratives of Gig Economy: An Indian HR Perspective (83–99), *NHRD Network Journal*, 15 (1).
Prince, A. (2021), Kerala Govt's Uber-Model Taxi Service to Ride on Reasonable Pricing, *Mathrubhumi.com*, September 25. Available at: https://englisharchives.mathrubhumi.com/features/specials/kerala-savari-kmtwwf-1.6033969
Punia, K. (2020), Future of Unemployment and the Informal Sector India, *Observer Research Foundation*, March 12. Available at: https://www.orfonline.org/expert-speak/future-of-unemployment-and-the-informal-sector-of-india-63190/
Rachmawati, R., Zakia, L., Lupita, A. and de Ruyter, A. (2021), Urban Gig Workers in Indonesia during Covid-19: The Experience of Online 'Ojek' Drivers (31–45), *Work Organisation, Labour & Globalisation*, 15(1).
Ray, A, (2019), Unrest in India's Gig Economy: Ola-Uber Drivers Strike and Worker Organisation10, *Futures of Work*, December 9. Available at: https://futuresofwork.co.uk/2019/12/09/unrest-in-indias-gig-economy-ola-uber-drivers-strikes-and-worker-organisation/
Refyne: Privacy Policy. Available at: https://refyne.co.in/privacy-policy.html
Romeo, N. (2021), Should Gig Work Be Government-Run? *The New Yorker*, March 23. Available at: https://www.newyorker.com/tech/annals-of-technology/should-gig-work-be-government-run
Saini, S. (2023), Rajasthan Outlines Plans for Gig Workers Welfare, *Hindustan Times*, April 27. Available at: https://www.hindustantimes.com/india-news/rajasthan-plans-welfare-cess-for-gig-workers-proposes-fine-up-to-1-crore-on-errant-aggregators-101682534795170.html
Sanzgiri, V. (2023), Big Win for Rajasthan Gig Workers? Gehlot Announces Gig Workers Welfare Act, *Medianama*, February 13. Available at: https://www.medianama.com/2023/02/223-rajasthan-announces-gig-workers-welfare-act-board/
Sapni, G. K. (2021), The Murky Waters of Kerala's Knowledge Economy Mission, *The Bastion*, September 24. Available at: https://thebastion.co.in/politics-and/the-murky-waters-of-keralas-knowledge-economy-mission/
Sasidharan, A. and Krishna, N. (2023), Platform Co-ops: Democratising the Digital Economy, *India Development Review*, January 20. Available at: https://idronline.org/article/livelihoods/platform-co-ops-democratising-the-digital-economy/
Saxena, A. (2022), Financial Services to Underserved Gig Workers, *YourStory*, July 15. Available at: https://yourstory.com/2022/07/httpsyourstorycom202207fintech-startup-karmalife-provides-financial-services-to-gig-workers
Scholz, T. and Calzada, I. (2021), Data Cooperatives for Pandemic Times, *Public Seminar*, April 19. Available at: https://publicseminar.org/essays/data-cooperatives-for-pandemic-times/
Shroff, K. (2021), Inside the Winter of Discontent for India's Gig Workers, *The Wire*, December 26. Available at: https://thewire.in/labour/india-gig-workers-protests-pil

Snider, L. (2018), Enabling Exploitation: Law in the Gig Economy (563–577), *Critical Criminology*, 26.

Soriano, C. R. R. & Cabanes, J. V. A. (2020), Entrepreneurial Solidarities: Social Media Collectives and Filipino Digital Platform Workers (1–11), *Social Media + Society*, April-June

Spain: The Rider's Law, New Regulation on Digital Platform Work (2021), European Agency for Safety and Health at Work, Policy Case Study, 1–12. Available at: https://osha.europa.eu/sites/default/files/2022-01/Spain_Riders_Law_new_regulation_digital_platform_work.pdf

Standing, G. (2011), *The Precariat: The New Dangerous Class*, Bloomsbury Academic, London, NY

The Code on Social Security 2020: Addressing the Key Changes and Their Impact (2023), *Ahlwat & Associates*, February 8. Available at: https://www.legal500.com/developments/thought-leadership/the-code-on-social-security-2020-addressing-the-key-changes-and-their-impact/

Urban Company (UC) Women Workers all Night Strike Against Proposed Policy Changes (2021), *Gauri Lankesh News*, December 21. Available at: https://gaurilankeshnews.com/urban-company-uc-women-workers-all-night-strike-against-proposed-policy-changes/

Vasudevan. K. and Keung Chan, N. (2022), Gamification and Work Games: Examining Consent and Resistance among Uber Drivers (866–886), *New Media & Society* 24(4).

Wiessner, D., Bose, N. and Shepardson, D. (2022), Biden Labor Proposal Shakes Up Gig Economy that Relies on Contractors, *Reuters*, October 12. Available at: https://www.reuters.com/world/us/new-biden-labor-rule-would-make-contractors-into-employees-2022-10-11/

Wood, A. J., Graham, M., Lehdonvirta, V. and Hjorth, I. (2019), Good Gig, Bad Gig: Autonomy and Algorithmic Control in the Global Gig Economy (56–75), *Work, Employment & Society*, 33(1).

Wood, A. J. and Lehdonvirta, V. (2021), Antagonism beyond Employment: How the 'Subordinated Agency' of Labour Platforms Generates Class Conflicts in the Remote Gig Economy (1369–1396), *Socio-Economic Review*, 19(4).

World Employment and Social Outlook: The role of Digital Labour Platforms in Transforming the World of Work (2021:1–13), International Labour Union, Executive Summary. Available at: https://www.ilo.org/wcmsp5/groups/public/@dgreports/@dcomm/documents/publication/wcms_771672.pdf

Zizek, S. (2009), *First as Tragedy, then as Farce*, Verso, London & NY

Other References

Arora, N. & Toopran, S. (2022), Podcast. S5Ep119: Lending to India's Gig Economy with Badal Malick of KarmaLife.AI. Transfin.Long Shorts with Nikhil Arora and Sharath Toopran, April 28. Available at: https://transfin.substack.com/p/s5-ep119-lending-to-indias-gig-economy-33b#details

RSA Animate, First as Tragedy, then as Farce. Available at: https://www.youtube.com/watch?v=hpAMbpQ8J7g

6 Cloud, Data Centres and the Politics of Infrastructure

John Durham Peters (2015) in his book *The Marvellous Clouds* has argued for our need to revert to the original meaning of the word 'media' that was bound up with elemental nature – earth, water, sky and fire. He has argued that our need to consider this older meaning of the word has been precipitated by ubiquitous digital media that, in many real ways, structures the environments in which we live in and provides us with the meanings with which we understand our physical and natural environments. A good example of this planetary-scale capacity to structure, order and manage the world is the extraordinary powers vested in Cloud centres to sort, manage and control the flows of ubiquitous data across multiple sectors. Peters is pessimistic about such global infrastructures that by no means exist to further human freedoms but are fundamentally about the expansion of control for population management. The scale and embrace of this enterprise requires us to understand this infrastructure as media, in the elemental sense of its meaning. 'When our environment is so technically saturated, when our crafts have altered the air and the deep—when Google, for instance, is a major ecosystem actor—we need to understand the intelligent contrivances, the technologies and techniques…, that have made humans the planetary hegemon in recent millennia. New media invite the deepest and oldest questions of social theory. Ubiquitous computing invites us to turn from the urgency of the message to the nature of media (and the media of nature)' (2015:8). What makes such infrastructure unique is that it shares infrastructural continuities with successive developments linked to digital technology – from IT corridors and Free Trade Zones to Big Tech that are constitutive of 'Extrastatecraft', a term coined by Keller Easterling to connote the manner in which such infrastructure now plays a commanding role in sorting, sifting, storing and managing both personal and non-personal data with and without the support of the State and most often without any meaningful consent from the billions of data generators. What I have tried to explore in this chapter is the power of these data organisations but also the role played by the Indian State in relinquishing control over these data centres despite the rhetoric of Made in India and data sovereignty. Easterling (2014:33–34) highlights the many initiatives and special incentives

DOI: 10.4324/9781003491705-7

granted to companies in Free Trade Zones that have enabled them to circumvent extant laws related to labour, the environment and taxation and indulge in economic practices, dispositional behaviours and business practices that would invite penalties for older brick and mortar companies that belong to the analogue era.

> As a legal and economic instrument, the zone presides over a cocktail of enticements and legal exemptions that are sometimes mixed together with domestic civil laws, sometimes manipulated by business to create international law, and sometimes adopted by the nation in its entirety. Incentives vary in every location but might include: holidays from incomes or sales tax, dedicated utilities like electricity or broadband, deregulation of labor laws, prohibition of labor unions and strikes, deregulation of environmental laws, streamlined customs and access to cheap imported or domestic labour, cheap land and foreign ownership of property, exemptions from import/export duties, foreign language services, or relaxed licensing requirements

While some of these provisions such as access to cheap labour may not apply to the everyday functioning of what are labour-lite industries, the other provisions contained in this quotation also apply to data and cloud centres. Submarine cable centres are also a part of digital infrastructure that operates both in the 'Cloud' and 'Undersea'.

Submarine Cable Infrastructure

Billions of dollars have been invested in infrastructures that undergird the platform economy in India. In 2022, there were 15 international submarine cables that landed in 14 landing stations in Mumbai, Chennai, Tuticorin, Cochin and Trivandrum along with domestic submarine cables that connect the subcontinent with outlying islands such as Andaman and Nicobar. Apart from BSNL's interests in these operations, the majority of cables and cable landing sites are owned by the private sector and companies such as TCL, Jio, Vodafone, Airtel, Sify and others (Chattopadhyaya:2022). Big Tech companies such as Google (Alphabet), Facebook (Meta), Microsoft and Amazon are either sole owners or part owners of cables that link India to the rest of the world (e.g. the Airtel/Meta cable partnership, Google's ownership of the Blue–Raman cable connecting Italy and India (Bannerman:2020)), Critical infrastructure that has become key to the 'lit capacity' – bandwidth capacity in optical fibre networks that has become increasingly important to Big Tech organisations (Aparna:2023). These companies have become by far the most dominant users of undersea cable capacity and are fast becoming the primary financiers of submarine cables and in that process taking over the ownership of submarine cables from traditional telecommunications companies

(Mims:2022). Blum and Baraka (2022) in an article on Big Tech investments in submarine cables to Africa have observed the slow and steady attempts to control this market.

> Alphabet held nearly $150 billion in cash in the third quarter of 2021, more than the GDP of all but four African nations — to overbuild capacity, allowing room for future growth. And it can connect markets ahead of any clear immediate demand — an especially powerful lever in Africa. Once the cable is up and running, Google's network managers can prioritise Google's own data traffic, ensuring the performance and reliability of their cloud services — while using that reliability as the services' key selling point.

These undersea cable networks that carry 95 per cent of total data traffic are critical to overseas data and cloud centres and it is clear that Big Tech is investing significantly in an infrastructure that in 2022 carried 66 per cent of data traffic generated by these companies. Csernatoni (2022), in an article on the geopolitics of submarine cable, highlights the specific reasons for Big Tech control of this infrastructure given their involvement in the production, storage, circulation of data and their interest in the ownership of key vectors and the vertical and horizontal ownership of the entire data business. 'While telecom companies are focused on their end customers, hyperscalers and content providers aim to keep connectivity between their data server farms that form their cloud services, while allowing data transfers to function without disruptions. In this respect, **'clouds' are not only in the sky, but also and mostly undersea** and dependent on the physicals infrastructure of cables. Instead of relying on a supply chain operated by a consortia of big carriers many dependent on regional and national jurisdictions, cloud suppliers want to deploy their own subsea links'. Manish Jha and Rishi Jha's (2022:146) article *Data Centres in Navi Mumbai* in the edited volume *Data Centres as Infrastructure* provides an extensive introduction to the deliberate infrastructuralisation of this area under the aegis of the City and Industrial Development Corporation of Maharashtra (CIDCO) that enabled the development of extensive Information Tech Parks, Special Economic Zones and that led to massive investments by firms who were given special incentives. The fact there are submarine landing sites in and around this year was a major incentive for these cloud and data centres to invest in and site their operations in this area. A host of international submarine cable links – 12 out of the 20 in India are routed through Mumbai making it an attractive space for data industries such as data and cloud centres. Writing on the data centre, CtrLS notes that 'It hosts data of over a hundred clients including government departments,manufacturing companies, financial and banking organisations, insurance companies, public sector undertakings, e-commerce businesses, investment banking companies, Infotech companies, business solution consultants, power sector companies, multi-company brands, medial research organisations, infotainment industries, machinery and automobile giants, logistics companies, among many others'.

Data and Cloud Centres in India

Data centres and cloud services, supercomputers and high-speed links accompanied by data policies (such as the National Telecom Policy, 2012, MeghRaj Policy, 2014, Storage of Payments Systems Data, 2018, Draft e-Commerce Policy, 2019, Data Centre Park Policy, 2020) have led to this sector becoming critical to India's ambitions to become a multi-trillion-dollar economy. In September 2022, there were 138 data centres in India with a capacity of 870 MW that is projected to grow to 1,700 MW in 2025 (Pandey:2022). India's data centre market was valued at $4.35 bn in 2021 and was predicted to grow to $10.09 bn in 2027 (Singal:2023). There are essentially two types of data centres in India – colocation data centres where a number of companies share space for storing and running their IT services along with hyperscale colocation services typically run by a Big Tech company such as Amazon based on mega-power requirements and built-in scalability options. Cloud services, in particular, are now recognised as key intermediaries in data management, data storage, data applications and data services that have increasingly become vital to commercial platforms as well as to government projects such as Digital India and India Stack. In the space of a decade, payment interfaces such as UPI on mobile phones authenticated by Aadhar have become the means for digital transactions in India for the bulk of the population. These foundational platforms have spawned an ecology of fintech solutions and start-ups involved in the provisioning of goods and services within this ecosystem. The great variety of transactional platforms that cater to the need for e-commerce add to the generation of data that in turn require the infrastructures of data and cloud. So, in that sense, the data transactions generated on Swiggy, Zomato, Uber and Ola are stored in third-party data centres. In the case of Swiggy, data is generated in their partnership with restaurants, delivery partners, management of orders, clients and payment and customer services. While Swiggy does have an internal, AI-driven data science platform that deals with internal workflows, their transactional data is stored on an Amazon Web Services (AWS) SageMaker platform. 'DSP is part of the larger Platform umbrella within Swiggy. The Platform group builds and supports other core components that DSP utilizes extensively. The Data Platform (DP) arm of the Platform runs the (AWS based) data lake which houses all of Swiggy's transactional and log data, manages data brokers that stream messages to/from various services' (Sathynarayana:2019). Similarly, Swiggy's subsidiary Supr Daily a grocery-ordering and delivery service based in Bangalore uses AWS for infrastructure provisioning, image recognition and inventory planning including Amazon Rekognition, Amazon Forecast and Amazon S3 storage service (AWS:2022). As Narayan (2022:923) has argued, cloud providers such as AWS set the 'basic technical and organisational preconditions' for the growth of the platform economy. *'The elasticity of cloud computing that enables new logics of scaling remains under theorised as an infrastructural forces of 21st century corporate expansion'* (912, emph. authors).

While the GoI has invested in its own cloud project – Meghraj – specifically to cater to the data needs generated via its many e-government initiatives, the National Informatics Centre offers Platform as Service (PaaS), Infrastructure as Service (IaaS), Software as Service (SaaS), Storage as Service among other services and has established data centres around the country. While there have been attempts to create an indigenous operating system, BharOS to compete with the Android OS, India remains dependent on Big Tech companies to build its platform infrastructures. BharOS is a fork of the Android Open Source Project that is owned by Google (See Kodali: 2023) and a key question is whether it can fare better than previous indigenous systems such as IndusOS that are now defunct (Bordoloi: 2023). While the GoI's approach to regulation has increasingly become shaped by the discourse of data nationalism, data localisation and data sovereignty (*Aatmanirbhar Bharat* – Self Reliant India), it is clear that the private sector and, in particular, Big Tech data companies are very closely integrated with the provisioning of both public and private data services. In fact, the evidence of numerous umbilical cord projects between Big Tech and GoI initiatives raises critical questions related to data privacy. Given all the delays in the legislation of a Data Protection Act, the export of personal data by companies falls under the purview of the Information Technology (Reasonable Security Practices and Procedures and Sensitive Personal Data or Information) Rules 2011 (SPDI Rules) that does not provide explicit guidelines or prohibits the transfer of personal data outside of India (See Mohanty et al.:2022). So, this then is a key issue with the entire India Stack project in India. There is at the moment at least, no law that is supportive of privacy and it would seem that by default the GoI thinks it owns data that is generated by its users – data that they think that they can share with startups in fintech and other areas without getting any explicit consent from those who generate data in the interests of economic growth. This is bound to become an issue in the future given the exponential increase in Aadhar-based everyday authentications that has become the key to the enactments of transactional citizenship in India.

Public–Private Cloud Partnerships

What are some examples of these public–private cloud partnerships? The MeitY has empanelled 19 cloud service providers who have cleared security certification to provide basic, advanced and managed cloud services including AWS, Hewlett Packard, Google and Microsoft among others to provide cloud services to government departments (See The Economic Times, 2017).

Table 6.1 MeitY Empanel CSPs

MeitY Empanel CSP's Basic Cloud Services offering details with Data Centre Location								
Sr. No.	*Cloud Service Provider*	*Data Centre Location*		*Deployment Models*			*STQC Audit Status*	*Empanelment Validity*
		For Public Cloud and VPC	*For GCC*	*Public Cloud*	*VPC*	*GCC*		
1	Amazon Internet Services Pvt. Limited	1) Mumbai-03	NO	YES	YES	NO	Audited	24/10/2023
2	Bharat Sanchar Nigam Limited (BSNL)	1) Ahmedabad-01 2) Faridabad-01	1) Ahmedabad-01 2) Faridabad-01	YES	YES	YES	Audited	12/09/2023
3	CtrlS Data Centers Limited	1) Hyderabad-01 2) Navi Mumbai-01	1) Hyderabad-01 2) Navi Mumbai-01	YES	YES	YES	Audited	12/09/2023
4	Cyfuture India Private Limited	1) Noida-01 2) Jaipur-0l	1) Noida-01 2) Jaipur-01	YES	YES	YES	Audited	12/09/2023
5	ESDS Software solution Pvt. Limited	1) Nashik-01 2) Mumbai-01 3) Bengaluru-01	1) Nashik-01 2) Mumbai-01 3) Bengaluru-01	YES	YES	YES	Audited	17/09/2023
6	Google Cloud India Pvt Ltd	1) Mumbai-01 2) Noida-01	NO	YES	YES	NO	Audited	31/01/2024
7	IBM India Private Limited	1) Chennai-01	NO	YES	YES	NO	Audited	25/02/2024
8	ITI Limited	1) Bengaluru-01	1) Bengaluru-01	YES	YES	YES	Audited	25/02/2024
9	Jio Platforms Limited	1) Mumbai-01 2) $\text{Jamnagar}_{(\text{IDC8})}$-01	YES	YES	YES	YES	Audited	04/12/2023
		1) Nagpur-01 2) Jamnagar-01	NO	YES	YES	NO	Audited	14/03/2026

10	Microsoft Corporation (India) Private Limited	1) Chennai-01 2) Mumbai-01 3) Pune-01	NO	YES	YES	NO	Audited	12/09/2023
11	Netmagic IT Services Private Limited	1) Mumbai-02 2) Bengaluru-02	1) Mumbai-02 2) Bengaluru-02	YES	YES	YES	Audited	12/09/2023
12	Nxtra Data Limited	1) Bengaluru-01 2) Noida-01	1) Bengaluru-01 2) Noida-01	YES	YES	YES	Audited	24/10/2023
13	Oracle India Pvt. Ltd	1) Navi Mumbai-01 2) Hyderabad-01	NO	YES	YES	NO	Audited	31/01/2024
14	Pi Datacenters Pvt. Ltd.	1) Guntur-01	1) Guntur-01	YES	YES	YES	Audited	13/12/2024
15	RailTel Corporation of India Limited	1) Gurugram-01 2) Secunderabad-01	1) Gurugram-01 2) Secunderabad-01	YES	YES	YES	Audited	02/02/2024
16	Sify Technologies Limited	1) Bengaluru-01 2) Navi Mumbai-01	1) Bengaluru-01 2) Navi Mumbai-01	YES	YES	YES	Audited	12/09/2023
17	Tata Communications Limited	1) Bengaluru-01 2) Mumbai-01 3) New Delhi-01	1) Mumbai-01 2) New Delhi-01	YES	YES	YES	Audited	12/09/2023
18	Webwerks India Pvt. Limited	1) Mumbai-01 2) Pune-01 3) Noida-01	1) Mumbai-01 2) Pune-01 3) Noida-01	YES	YES	YES	Audited	17/09/2023
19	Yotta Infrastructure Solutions Pvt. Ltd.	1) Navi Mumbai-01 2) Guntur-01	1) Navi Mumbai-01 2) Guntur-01	YES	YES	YES	Audited	01/12/2025

Source: https://www.meity.gov.in/content/gi-cloud-meghraj

The more intriguing and worrying development is the integration of the GoI's cloud storage system into Google's Android in December 2022, enabling deep connections between Aadhar data and DigiLocker and the Android operating system (Sharwood: 2022). Nishant (2022), in an article on Amazon's investment in its second infrastructure region in India, has described this global market leader in cloud technology's very close links to the GoI. 'The company has smartly manoeuvered the state policy and sees governments and public departments as a big growth opportunity in India. It has tied up with various Central and State ministries to innovate for the delivery of public services. Last year, it collaborated with the NITI Aayog and Intel to launch the Frontier Technologies Cloud Innovation Centre in the think tank's Delhi office. AWS stands to gain from its engagement with both ends of the spectrum—with the government as the facilitator, and startups, industry experts and enterprises as beneficiaries. Similarly, the company has taken its quantum computing service, Amazon Braket, to a select group of scientists through the Quantum Computing Applications Lab in a partnership with MeitY. The company captains feel that the massive infrastructure that the government has at its disposal needs technology adoption at an unprecedented scale for India to become a digital economy which, in turn, is a huge opportunity for the company'. In 2022, AWS launched its second cloud infrastructure region in India in Hyderabad (the first was in Mumbai in 2016) with an investment of US$4.4 billion. This infrastructure region will include a cluster of data centres located in three 'Availability Zones' along with investments in Local Centres in Chennai, Bengaluru and Kolkata in addition to 33 Amazon CloudFront edge centres that are located close to data companies (See Deutscher:2022).

Data Centre Policy

India currently is in the process of becoming a major hub for data centres and a number of states in India including Telangana, Tamilnadu, Uttar Pradesh and Bengal are easing opportunities for the acquisition of land, obtaining environmental and other clearances and investing in infrastructures such as power and electricity supplies, fibre optics, water supply, etc. that are required for the functioning of data and cloud centres. The Draft Data Centre Policy, 2020 issued by MeitY identifies some of the challenges facing this industry including complex clearance procedures, the high cost of power and limited submarine cable connectivity (1.6). The policy recognises the need for data centres to be granted 'Infrastructure Status' on par with the Railways and Power sectors, rationalise clearances for setting up of regional Data Centre Parks and establish

> i. Common service ducts and utility corridors for enabling proliferation of Optical Fibre Cables and dark fibre for the Data Centre operations and ensuring sharp reduction in downtime due to fibre cuts. ii. Sharing of active infrastructure by enhancing the scope of Infrastructure Providers

(IP) and promoting and incentivizing deployment of common sharable, passive as well as active, infrastructure.

(5.2...2.1)

To reiterate, the Data Centre Policy recommends that this sector be granted infrastructure status, encourages states to incentivise this sector via an incentivisation scheme, establish a favourable ecosystem for the operation of data centres, set up four Data Centre Economic Zones and promote indigenous technology development, R&D and capacity building (See Chaudhary: 2023 and TRAI:2021).

Land for Data and Cloud Centres

Given the priority that this sector has been granted, there is no shortage of venture capitalists investing in data centres and cloud computing infrastructures in India. A number of venture capitalists like the NY-based Blackstone Group (LuminaCloudInfra) (Nandy:2022), CapitaLand India Trust, local (Hiranandani – also owns Yotta Data Services, Times Property and Adani Group) and global real estate companies such as Prologis, Colliers, Savills and Cushman and Wakefield are involved in the acquisition of land and construction of data

centres – both large colocation, hyperscale and Tier II edge data centres.

They offer a range of services from market entry studies and land acquisition to construction, investments and private equity. 'Savills India Land Services for Data Centres undertakes land transactions for Data Centre properties on behalf of individuals, developers, funds, government & government undertaking companies, corporates, trust, and private companies. Our team assists you in identifying, evaluating, and buying land' (Savills). The Assetz Property Group was involved in 2023 in selling a 47-acre land parcel (described as freehold land) in Thane to the Singapore-based Digital Edge for Rs. 806 crore ($97.2 mn) for their first data centre in India (Moises:2023).

A 2021 report from the real estate company Cushman & Wakefield that specialises in acquiring land for hyperscale and other data centres includes information on investments and acquisitions in the local data centre market in India.

The Telangana Government and Data Centres

Such investments are in addition to the multi-billion-dollar investments made by the three big, hyperscale services – AWS, Microsoft Azure (MZ) and Google Cloud (GC) whose data centre footprint criss-crosses the Indian subcontinent. The report highlights Mumbai (44 % of the data centre market) and Bengaluru (25%) and the growth of Chennai that has the second-best

Figure 6.1 Cushman & Wakefield.

undersea cable connectivity (five cables) after Mumbai and significant investments by AWS, MZ, GC and Tencent, a sixth $400 million, 8,100-km cable constructed by NEC Corporation – the Myanmar/Malaysia-India-Singapore Transit (MIST) (See Rohit:2022) along with other investments in data centres by Yotta, CtrLS, Princeton Digital, STT and Nxtgen (5). Cushman & Wakefield were involved in acquiring land for Microsoft in Hyderabad – a total of 110 acres in Chandanvelly, Ellikatta and Kottur for setting up data centres that cost 450 crores. This land is in addition to Microsoft's strong presence in Hyderabad – its 55-acre campus in Gachibowli (Bharadwaj:2022). AWS too has a strong data footprint in Telangana. In 2022, the government of Telangana allocated 50 acres in the Electronic City, Raviryal, 48 acres at Meerkhanpet and 33 acres at Chandanvelly, Rangrareddy District to AWS (BusinessLine:2020) as a part of its $3.71 billion investment in India. The Telangana government, like other state governments, has decided to migrate its e-government data (generated by 33 departments and 289 organisations) to the cloud in line with its Cloud Adoption Framework beginning with the Aarogyasri Health Care Trust (Aarogyasri), the Greater Hyderabad Municipal Corporation (GHMC), and the Telangana State Department of Information Technology, Electronics, and Communications (ITE&C) that will move its data from on-premises to AWS cloud (Lele:2022).

> The growing demand for digital services has increased the volume of public service operational data managed by Telangana. Aarogyasri, a state organization facilitating health insurance implementation, ITE&C, the department charged with using IT to achieve effective and efficient governance, sustainable economic development, and inclusive social development, and GHMC outgrew their on-premises data centers. For example, the Aarogyasri Scheme, a free health care program serving approximately 29 million people living below the poverty line in Telangana, experienced quadruple growth in usage year over year for the past decade, and its co-located space in the Telangana State Data Center could not keep pace with the demand and lacked the capacity to support the program's growth. GHMC, which provides municipal services for Hyderabad's 6.9 million residents, needed to improve the availability and scalability of its Oracle E-Business Suite enterprise resource planning (ERP) software so that it could efficiently perform operations like payroll and support new applications and citizen services in future. ITE&C, which oversees eOffice—the file management system used by all 33 government districts to complete daily operational tasks—also needed to prevent downtime and reduce its steep ongoing compute costs.
>
> (SME Street:2022)

I would have liked to from a critical political economy perspective explore the nature of land acquisition by these data centres and real estate intermediaries like Cushman & Wakefield although there is very little documentation that is publicly available. The acquisition of land for Special Economic Zones (See Fish:2011, Misra:2019, Faustina:2022) and IT corridors have been contentious precisely because common land has been allocated to these sectors often for below-the-market prices and ordinary people have been evicted to make way for such parks. State governments, such as in Telangana, offer captive, dedicated land – Data Centre Campuses for the hosting of multiple data centres. There are however questions that remain – what processes, apart from technical, are followed in the acquisition of large parcels of land in India today for the data industry? Are land acquisition processes deliberative and do they include the involvement of those who have been evicted? While the concept of 'eminent domain' has been invoked by the State to take over private land for infrastructural projects, are such concepts being used to procure space for hyperscale and other data centre projects in contemporary India? What strategies are used by global real estate companies in the data centre industry in

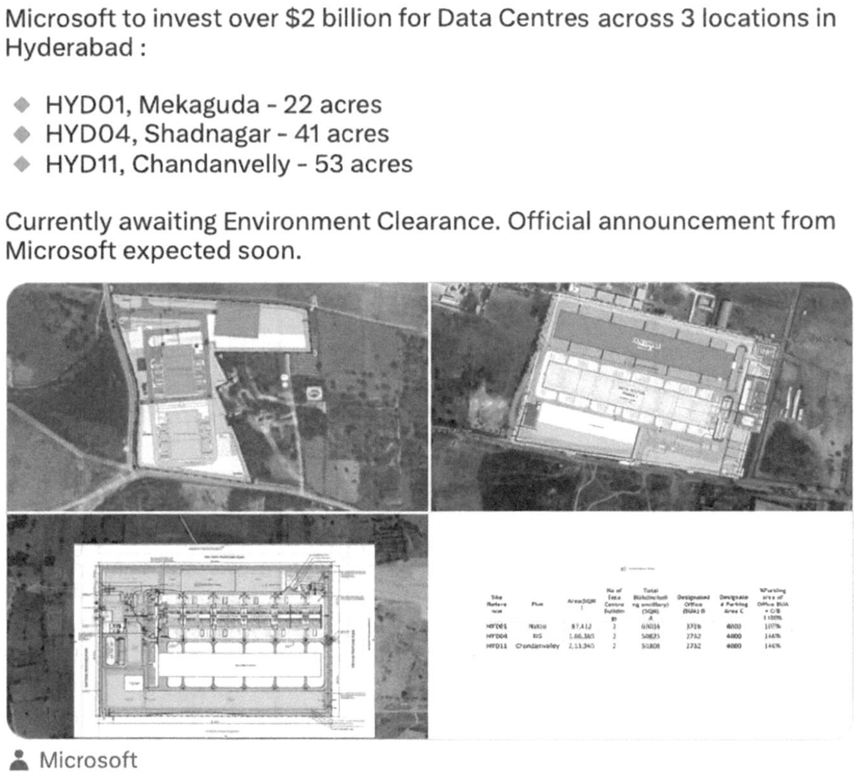

Figure 6.2 Microsoft's Plans for Date Centres in Hyderabad.

India and who do they ally with locally to clinch land deals? In other words, who are the winners and losers in infrastructural projects?

There are 12 colocation data centres located in Hyderabad including Iron Mountain data Centres HYD-1, Sify Hyderabad, CtrlS Data Centre, Kedia data Centre, Nettlinx, Tata Communications Hyderabad, Net4 Data Centre, Reliance IDC, Railtel Corporation of India Ltd., Kloudya Godavari, STT Hyderabad DC 1 and BSNL-SIS Data Centre (Hyderabad Data Centres). 'Hyderabad today roughly has an IT design power load of 30MW capacity with a data centre built up space of over seven lakh sq ft primarily concentrated in HITEC City and Budvel. About 80 per cent of the built up space is utilised by 5,864 racks/units. The city is expected to see an addition of 8MW in 2021, followed by 29 MW each for 2022 and 2023' (Raj:2021).

The Consequences of Infrastructure

Data centre infrastructure typically consists of four sectors – 1) network Infrastructure that includes servers, networking equipment such as modems and routers, firewall security and cabling systems, 2) the physical infrastructure that includes buildings, power and cooling technologies, etc, 3) computing infrastructures including the racks and 4) storage infrastructure for internal and external storage of data and backup data. Arguably, the technological infrastructure associated with cloud computing and data centres is just one part of the story. Understanding the infrastructure requires an expansive imaginary that enables us to see the integrated, interconnections between physical spaces and entities such as land and buildings brimming with servers on hundreds of racks with a multiplicity of infrastructural connectivities from the outside – fibre optic cables, power and water supplies piped through cables, pipes and grids. In other words, the infrastructural 'inside' is always connected to and shaped by the infrastructural 'outside' – roads, transport, labour, bureaucracy, rules and regulations – a process that results in 'land parcels' being transformed into cloud and data centres. Data and cloud centres begin their life in strategic plan documents created by key actors – the state, corporations, private investment firms and their infrastructural enactment is typically the end process in a long cycle of project development that often stretches over seven years. As Ribes and Finholt (2009: 377–378) have argued 'Infrastructure stretches across multiple scales of action' that involve technology, work and institutions. More than two decades ago, Graham and Marvin (2001:11) in their landmark study *Splintering Urbanism* had made a case for a 'spatial imaginary' that was required to understand the 'socio-techncial geometries of power' that infrastructure networks possess and reinforce. They argued for a need to see urban infrastructure networks *as a whole* and that included streets, transport, telecommunication grids and energy systems (See Graham and Marvin:2022). Theresa Enright (2022:102), in a special issue of the *Journal of Urban Technology* dedicated to revisiting the study *Splintering Urbanism*, argues that 'a focus on the "imaginary"' qualities of infrastructure is frequently more obfuscating than revelatory. Spatial imaginaries are by definition partial, contingent and misrepresentative. They are formed in dialectical relation to 'real' urban conditions and connected to one another through multiple and contested semantic chains of association and disassociation. While it is certainly difficult to account for 'infrastructural complexity', given the many contingent factors that impact any given infrastructure, it is nevertheless necessary to ground this imaginary in the real, in context, and engage with the materialities that are at the core of infrastructures such as data and cloud centres. Infrastructures are mediated by the visible and the invisible. It is this latter – 'the invisible' – that is bound to be incomplete in any work on infrastructures precisely because these involve an understanding of the hidden transcripts, information on infrastructural decision-making and the allocation and flow of resources, in particular, financial that often is a grey area. Even the real material impact that infrastructural projects can have – for example, uninterrupted electricity supplies to data centres versus the consequences from the outages that people in Indian cities frequently face, the depletion of groundwater in farmlands close to data centres and other high energy consumption industries and the environmental impacts irrespective of data centres' commitment to greening, green energy, etc. The environmental impact of data centres in India is yet to become a focus for investigation given the commitment by states and competition to provide companies the best incentives that include unfettered supply to energy – electricity supplies and water for cooling in a country in which 600 million people face severe water access constraints and in which 21 cities including Tier 1 cities such as Chennai, Hyderabad, Bengaluru and Delhi exhausted groundwater resources in 2021. Choudhary (2022) highlights the severity of the problem and the role played by data centres 'Pali, a small city in Rajasthan with a total population of about 230,000 faces water crisis every year. So much so that the city administration is forced to fetch water in special trains from the neighbouring city of Jodhpur. Barely 300 km away, however, are a few data centres in Jaipur, where the daily water consumption supersedes the entire city of Pali'. While some data centres in India have invested in solar and other green energy sources, they are under no pressure to go 'green'. In fact, data centres have been spared from following green policies that apply to other industries. The fact remains that 59.1 per cent of the electricity is based on fossil fuels, 51 per cent of which comes from coal. Jena (2022), writing in *The Wire*, observes that in Maharashtra that accounts for 40 per cent of India's installed data centres, the total electricity generated from fossil fuel sources, mainly coal is 78 per cent. Since the country expects to double its installed capacity by the end of 2023, its reliance on coal- and fossil fuel–generated electricity is bound to keep expanding. This energy-intensive industry has been given preferential treatment globally and there is secrecy related to data centres and their consumption of energy. In the USA, Google, for instance, treats its water consumption as a trade secret and it was only after legal struggles with conservation groups and local utilities that it was disclosed in 2019. Google was granted 2.3 billion gallons of water specifically for data centres in three states (Sattiraju:2020). While some Big Tech companies such as Microsoft have invested in solar and other types of green energy, for the most part, data centres in India rely on energy generated by fossil fuels. This stands in marked contrast to the situation in Sweden where following the announcement from the Head of Stockholm Data Parks to phase out fossil fuels in Stockholm by 2040. There are plans to commodify and pipe the residual heat energy (waste heating) from data centres as forms of heating in residential areas. There are similar initiatives in Finland (see Velkova:2021). For a more detailed article on sustainable data centres, see Shuja et al.: 2016).

The political economy of land acquisitions in relation to evictions of the urban and rural poor have been investigated although the long-term consequences of such evictions require more study. Both sustainability and land evictions are in key ways the other side of the story of Digital India. Since the various infrastructural projects linked to Digital India are seen as critical to India's emergence as a knowledge superpower, there is little critique of its impact on people, livelihoods and the environment. If water consumption by data centres has an impact on the local water table, this is bound to be further amplified by the 100 smart-city projects and other mega-development projects that are part of the neoliberal economic agenda adopted by the government of India. The National Industrial Corridor Corporation (NICDC), India's flagship infrastructure programme is involved in the development of 11 infrastructure corridors including four smart industrial cities in Dholera (Gujarat), Shendra Bidkin (Maharashtra), Vikram Udyogpuri (MP) and the Integrated Industrial Township in Greater Noida (UP) for which land allotment has been fast-tracked (Singh:2022). There is certainly evidence that larger numbers of people are being evicted to make space for smartcities. There are estimates that 22,360 people were evicted for the smart cities project out of which there were 32 cases of forced eviction. The Kashi Vishwanath Corridor project linked to a smartcity in Varanasi, UP led to the eviction of 4500 people and the demolition of shops and residential complexes and inadequate compensation (Kumar:2020). Sai Balakrishnan in an article on the links between politicians and real estate in Bengaluru has remarked on the role played by the Bangalore Development Authority in becoming the monopoly acquirer and developer of land in 1976 that was based on amendments to the Karnataka Land Reforms Act that prohibited any purchase of land by non-agriculturalists and companies. The BDA invoked eminent domain to acquire these lands, proceed to develop infrastructural services and allocate land and create unauthorised layouts on the basis of multiple informalities involving both political leaders and trade unions (Balakrishnan:2021, 2086–87). Michael Levian's (2012:946) article on land question in the *Journal of Peasant Studies* highlights the processes of dispossession in Rajasthan 'Mahindra World City, a multi-purpose 'integrated industrial city' 25 km from Jaipur, which is supposed to include the largest IT-SEZ in India. To facilitate this project by the real estate subsidiary of the $7 billion Mahindra and Mahindra Company in partnership with RIICO, the Rajasthan government (through the Jaipur Development Authority) acquired 3,000 acres of land in 9 villages, of which 2,000 acres was privately owned farmland and 1,000 acres was common grazing land (officially owned by the government). As government land, the latter was transferred to the company with no compensation to the surrounding villages that were highly dependent on the livestock economy it supported' (See also Chatterjee:2012). It is fascinating that this politics of dispossession was perfected in the era of Empire. The Land Acquisitions Act of 1894 enabled state enclosures of privately owned land. David Johnson (2010:106) in an article on the building of New Delhi highlights the fact that under this act, no appeals could be made on the loss of land. Those who were not granted any compensation were small cultivators who did not own land but who worked in agriculture and in vocations such as masons, carpenters and blacksmiths, a reality that has persisted into the post-colonial era.

Microsoft's investment in a data centre in Chandanvally is in itself in the Chandanvally Industrial Park that is a 1,569-acre facility (NewsTap). In a country such as India where land has become premium, land acquisition is just the beginning of the infrastructural moment. When land is bought outside of the city, massive investments have to be made to ensure connectivity – to power supply, in particular, that is critical to data centre processes and the cooling that is required for optimum air flows and is critical for rack/server performance. Data halls often house 15–20,000 servers that generate massive amounts of heat that need to be cooled down. In other words, there are other, more prosaic infrastructures that are critical to the sustainability of cloud infrastructures and data centres such as power supply. In India, there is a shortage of power – and diesel generators were used for backup, although increasingly, these companies are investing in non-renewables such as solar. In 2018, Microsoft invested in its first solar power deal in Bengaluru that will supply 80 per cent of its electricity needs at its Bengaluru office (Rajeshwari:2018). Similarly, Amazon has invested in three solar farms in Rajasthan with a 420 MW capacity (Economic Times). Subsidised and duty-free tariff on electricity is guaranteed by some states such as Maharashtra to encourage data centres to invest. In Telangana, data centres are serviced by dual-power grid networks and power is available at subsidised rates. Water too is a premium commodity in India – and it is not clear if the large supplies of water required to maintain these facilities are a drain on groundwater that is essential to local farming and survival.

Skirting Legislative Requirements

Another infrastructural obstacle is the Indian bureaucracy and the multiple laws that are in place for building permission. The suite of laws that need to be negotiated and given approval for is quite extensive. An environmental assessment report (2022:1.8–1.9) prepared by Microsoft for buildings on its campus in Gachibowli, Hyderabad *Environmental Impact Assessment For Building 3 and a Multilevel Car Parking Construction Project by Microsoft India (R & D) Pvt. Limited, Sy. No. 210/1 and 203/P, Manikonda Jagir, Gachibowli, Rajendranagar (M), Rangareddy District, Telangana State Project/Activity-8 (b), Category 'B1'* (2022) lists 38 rules and regulations that fall under Environmental Rules & Regulations including the following two:

- Minimum Wages Act, 1948.
- The Minimum Wages Rules, 1950 & The Minimum Wages Rules, 1950 (State Rules) (1.9)

While India does have a reputation/space/unofficial opportunities for the 'negotiation' of such rules, the Telangana government's Data Centre Policy, 2016 (1–28) clearly identifies non-fiscal incentives for data centres investing in the state. These include the following:

1 Data Centre firms are exempt from the purview of the Telangana Pollution Control Act, except in respect of IT parks/IT SEZ campuses with built up area over 20,000 sq.mt., special permissions need to be taken from SEIAA under MoEF.

2 Data Centre firms are exempt from the purview of statutory power cuts.
3 Data Centre firms are exempt from inspections under the following Acts and the Rules framed thereunder, barring inspections arising out of specific complaints. These units are permitted to file self-certificates, in the prescribed formats.
   - The Factories Act, 1948
   - The Maternity Benefit Act, 1961
   - The Telangana Shops & Establishments Act, 1988
   - The Contract Labour (Regulation & Abolition) Act,1970
   - The Payment of Wages Act, 1936
   - The Minimum Wages Act, 1948
   - The Employment Exchanges (Compulsory Notification of Vacancies) Act, 1959
4 General permission for three shift operations with women working in the night.

(26)

The abeyance of these rules, especially related to labour, has been a precondition for company investments in Special Economic Zones in India for over three decades. The key benefit for companies is the ability to recruit non-unionised labour for low wages and be able to hire and fire them at will, unlike the case of workers in blue-collar jobs in industry and manufacturing who often are unionised and enjoy rights. The fact that the rights of women in particular – maternity leave, wages, health and security – have been compromised through State fiat is of special concern. This lowering of worker's rights in the IT industry in India has been uniformly followed at an all-India level, been consistently applied by most if not all state governments and directly contributed to the creation of the category of 'gig' workers in the information industries. It has led to the complete dereliction of the responsibilities of platform intermediaries over their 'workers' who are often described as 'partners' not employees. The fact that the NITI Aayog report on gig workers celebrates the prospect of many millions of people working in gig work in India needs to be seen in the context of the precarity and insecurity of employment in a country where hundreds of thousands of people apply for government jobs. Work in the gig economy requires a worker with a smartphone and internet connectivity. Another issue is the leeway given to data centres to function outside of the purview of the Telangana Pollution Control Act. This facility and 'incentive' directly contravene the government's commitment to renewables, the greening of data centres, control of carbon footprint, etc. The fact that data centres located in government-owned data campuses will not need to abide by pollution rules that other industries and manufacturing units have to abide by highlights the competition for data centres and the willingness of governments to settle for the lowest common denominator. The government of Telangana's incentives include the following:

> The Data Centres Campus, in addition to hosting Government managed data storage facilities, shall cater to companies irrespective of their size and scale. Large companies interested in procuring Government land in the Data Centres Campus can set up their own facility. Small and medium companies, which specialize primarily in servers and racks, shall be provided with built up space equipped with basic infrastructure. Further, every player with presence in the Data Centres Campus shall be provided access to high speed fiber and continuous water supply for heavy duty cooling systems. Further, given the critical nature of data hosted at the Data Centres Campus and the importance of such a centralized facility, the Government shall, at its own cost, take up the responsibility of providing adequate security in and around the campus.
>
> (17)

Telangana is not the only state that has its own policy on data centres. A number of other states including UP, Haryana, Karnataka and Tamilnadu, among other states have established such policies. In Tamilnadu, 1,377 acres have been earmarked for the establishment of IT parks in Tier 1 and 2 cities by the Electronics Corporation of India (ELCOT) out of which the three largest allocations include 377 acres in Chennai's Sholinganallur district, 290 acres in Tirunelveli's Gangaikondan district and 245 acres in Madurai's Vadapalanji (TN DC 2021). State governments have used their infrastructure readiness as a key investment strategy. In the case of Tamilnadu, for example, the fact that 30 per cent of India's submarine cables that connect 264 stations are hosted in this state is an important point of differentiation with other states wooing foreign investments. In the neighbouring state of Karnataka, incentives include a capital subsidy of up to Rs 100 million, 10 per cent of land subsidy up to Rs 30 million, 100 per cent stamp duty exemption, concession on registration charges and 100 per cent exemption on land conversion charges. In Uttar Pradesh, the incentives go one step further: '100 per cent exemption of stamp duty on the first transaction (authority/landowner to data centre unit) and 50 per cent on the second transaction (data centre parks to data centre units) shall be available for purchase/lease of land by data centre units. A 100 per cent exemption on electricity duty for a period of 10 years post the commencement of commercial operation has been provided by the state government and dual grid power supply shall be made available on demand, at applicable charges. Additionally, the state government will ensure uninterrupted water supply to data centre units, both inside and outside the data centre park, for units in the area of the Industrial Area Development Authority' (Tele.Net; See also SR Insights for a comparison of inter-state data centre incentives).

Despite all these policies and investment incentives, the establishment of these data centres varies from state to state. A submission to the Telecoms Regulatory Authority of India highlights concerns including the following. 1) Policy multiplicity and confusion caused by this multiplicity including conflicting rules, regulations, incentives, norms, applicability and eligibility and variations between central and state government policies. 2) Implementation gaps caused by the lack of internal communication lags to state departments such as power, environment, pollution control boards, etc. 3) Significant issues with multiple bodies involved in clearances for data centres. 4) Despite policy commitments to the creation of one-step clearance windows, there is a need for multiple clearances resulting in delays in every aspect of the planning cycle. 5) Clearances for a greenfield project take 8–10 months. 6) These delays have a sectoral impact given high capital investments in land, buildings and infrastructure (ST Telemedia Global Data Centres:2022).

Theorising the Cloud on Earth

There is an overwhelming positivity about data and cloud centres in India that are seen as critical infrastructure to India's economic and political investments in the imagining of India as a global superpower. The Nehruvian commitment to heavy industry in the immediate aftermath of Independence and Modi's commitment to Digital India share in the vision of an instrumental, technological prowess and a commitment to building India sublime by subduing nature through investments in these temples of power. These are wholly positive endeavours that become celebrated mythologies of progress from which there is no turning back – only a way forward. Yet, one can argue that such mythologies of progress rather purposefully avoid any acknowledgement of impermanence and instabilities, the death of technology, the reality of cloud wastelands, cloud businesses moving from one country to another following favourable tax and other policies and the built-in obsolescence of server technologies (See Brodie & Velkova:2021). In India, there is an absence of discussions on cloud centres and, thereafter, on the consequences of such infrastructural assemblages on the environment, on the quality of groundwater and on its impact on local people and livelihoods after the decline or death of a data centre. In an article on the impermanent nature of data centres, Velkova includes a conversation with the Finnish data centre architect Juka Velkova (2019:5) who observed that 'data center companies are constantly re-evaluating the economic profitability of particular locations in synchrony with server replacement cycles and new legislative frameworks that come into force. Should tax regulations, electricity prices, legislation or geopolitical dynamics shift, even a hyper-sized data center like Google's in Finland or Facebook's in Sweden could make a corresponding move to a place with more economically favourable conditions within three years'. If this could happen in Sweden or Finland, surely it could also happen in India given the example of the migration of BPO services from India to countries where costs are even cheaper than in India.

Hogan and Vonderau (2019:1), issue editors of a special issue of *Culture Machine* dedicated to data centres, raise a number of questions for their contributors that begins with a situating of data centres as technical assemblages impacted by the complexity of its context.

> Taking data centers as technological apparatus as a starting point, this issue aims to discuss the cloud's philosophical, political, social, and environmental impacts and maps the diverse sociotechnical assemblages which emerge in the course of cloud infrastructuring processes. How do the infrastructures of the cloud integrate into local political contexts and industrial landscapes? How do the cloud's technologies relate to the emergence of specific forms of subjectivity, sociality, and urbanity? How can the barely visible and secret industrial spaces of the cloud be made visible and opened up for public engagement? And what does the study of data centres tell us about our current social moment?

Hogan and Vonderau raise an important question related to data centres as infrastructures – the fact that these are more than technological assemblages but are also socio-political constructs. Data centres in this sense are the end result of innumerable negotiations with bureaucracies, investors, regulatory authorities, local governments and other infrastructures such as electrical grids that fuel data centres. In the case of India, they are an essential material infrastructure that is core to the vision of Digital India, a cashless society, a modern, digitally charged superpower nation. Yet, this vision is built on a faulty understanding of infrastructure and the plenitude associated with data. There is a predominant sense in government-speak that data as the new wealth of the nation will lead to an erasure of disparities in a country in which mobile phones have become a critical intermediary to financial inclusion. While the many national-level digital mission projects have certainly contributed to the creation of digital natives among underprivileged groups, despite the best attempts to play down these divides, India is still home to one of the world's largest populations of the poor, underprivileged and malnourished. There are major disparities between lives and livelihoods in South India as opposed to North and Central India and no amount of investment in data centres will change that equation. That digital gig workers are part of the informal rather than formal economy is also being underplayed in Indian media and this has resulted in a general lack of awareness of where jobs are being generated, the quality of these jobs, job security in a context in which workers are dispensable and can easily be replaced. The fact that low-paid workers in service jobs are acting merely as foot-soldiers who can be turned into fodder by fickle Big Tech who are congenitally committed to seeking out the best returns for the lowest costs is a reality that the country will have to face in the not-too-distant future. India also now has a notoriety for actively being involved in the censoring of the internet, in being a world leader in internet shutdowns and the removal of social media posts that are deemed to be antithetical to the dreams of a Hindu nationalist state.

Tung-Hui Hu (2016) in *A Prehistory of the Cloud* reminds us that the materiality of the cloud is layered atop older infrastructures such as railway tracks, sewer lines and television circuits (xii). It is in other words, imbricated in these older infrastructures and also continuously engaged with bureaucracies and infrastructures that enable its seamless functioning. Yet, beyond the preferred vision of data cloud centres contributing to the re-envisioning of India as a knowledge superpower, it remains in Hu's words 'a resource-intensive, extractive technology that converts water and electricity into computational power, leaving a sizeable amount of environmental damage that it then displaces from sight' (146). This displacement from sight and the gaps that exist between what these cloud and data centres claim they do and what they actually do, in particular, their involvement in the exercise of rule setting and decision-making – in other words, governance – has been described by Easterling as 'Extrastatecraft'. Critically though, these centres also process data generated by gig workers who are involved in training the algorithms that in turn, oppress and condemn them to a life in the service to the data Gods.

Bibliography

A comparison of data centre policies adopted by the Indian states, S&R Assoicates, 2023. Available at: https://www.snrlaw.in/wp-content/uploads/2023/04/SR-Insights-Data-Centres-in-India-%E2%80%93-Opportunity-and-Incentives-Table.pdf

Amazon gets land for setting up data centres (2020), The Hindu Business Line, November 9. Available at: https://www.thehindubusinessline.com/info-tech/amazon-gets-land-for-setting-up-data-centres/article33060589.ece

Amazon plans 3 solar farms and 23 solar rooftop projects in India (2022), *The Economic Times*, September 21. Available at: https://economictimes.indiatimes.com/industry/renewables/amazon-drives-renewable-energy-push-with-71-new-projects/articleshow/94353163.cms

Aparna, R. (2023), Indian Undersea Cable Landing Stations Increased Capacity by 9x: Report, TelecomTalk, January 31. Available at: https://telecomtalk.info/indian-undersea-cable-landing-stations-capacity-9xtimes/671917/

Balakrishnan, S. (2021), Real estate politicians in India (2079–2094), *Urban Studies*, 58 (10).

Bannerman, N. (2020), Google to build $400m Blue-Raman Subsea Cable, Capacity, April 21. Available at: https://www.capacitymedia.com/article/29otc4cbu6due4nwemu4g/news/google-to-build-400m-blue-raman-subsea-cable

Bharadwaj, S. (2022), Microsoft to Invest Rs 15,000 Crore for its Largest Date Centre Region in Hyderabad, Times of India, March 8. Available at: https://timesofindia.indiatimes.com/city/hyderabad/ms-to-invest-15k-cr-for-its-largest-data-center-region-in-hyd/articleshow/90063667.cms

Blum, A. & Baraka, C. (2022), Sea Change, Rest of World: Reporting Global Tech Stories, May 10. Available at: https://restofworld.org/2022/google-meta-underwater-cables/

Bordoloi, P. (2023), India Govt Tech Disaster in the Making, AnalyticsIndiaMagazine, January 27. Available at: https://analyticsindiamag.com/bharos-will-it-meet-indusos-fate/

Brodie, P. & Velkova, J. (2021), Cloud ruins: Ericsson's Vaudreuil-Dorion data centre and infrastructural abandonment (869–885), *Information, Communication & Society*, 24 (6).

Chandanvally Industrial Park on 1,569 acres records investments of over Rs. 18,000 Cr (2023), *NewsTap*, February 24. Available at: https://www.newstap.in/telangana/chandanvelly-industrial-park-on-1569-acres-records-investments-of-over-rs-18000-cr-1464162

Chatterjee, I. (2012), Governance as 'performed', Governance as 'inscribed' (2443–2685), *Urban Studies*, 48 (12).
Chattopadhyaya, S. (2022), Cable Landing Stations in India, Submarine Cable Networks. Available at: https://www.submarinenetworks.com/stations/asia/india
Chaudhary, Y. (2023), The Rise of Data Centres in India Exploring the Growth and Challenges, Conventus Law, March 7. Available at: https://conventuslaw.com/report/the-rise-of-data-centers-in-india-exploring-the-growth-and-challenges/
Choudhary, L. (2022), Date Centres, Please Stop Drinking My Water, *s*, August 29. Available at: https://analyticsindiamag.com/data-centres-please-stop-drinking-my-water/
Csernatoni, R. (2022), The Geopolitics of Submarine Cables, the Infrastructure of the Digital Age, Italian Institute for International Political Studies, June 22. Available at: https://www.ispionline.it/en/publication/geopolitics-submarine-cables-infrastructure-digital-age-35516
Data Centre Policy (2020) (1–16), MeitY. Available at: https://www.meity.gov.in/writereaddata/files/Draft%20Data%20Centre%20Policy%20-%2003112020_v5.5.pdf
Data Centres Policy (2016:1–28), Information Technology, Electronics & Communications Department, Government of Telangana. Available at: https://www.telangana.gov.in/PDFDocuments/Telangana-Data-Centres-Policy.PDF
Deutscher, M. (2022), AWS Launches New Cloud Infrastructure Region in India, Will Invest $4.4B, SiliconAngle, November 22. Available at: https://siliconangle.com/2022/11/22/aws-launches-new-infrastructure-region-india/
Easterling, K. (2014), *Extrastatecraft: The Power of Infrastructure* Space, Verso, London & NY.
Enright. T. (2022), The Infrastructural Imagination (101–107), *Journal of Urban Technology*, 29(1).
Environmental Impact Assessment For Building 3 and Multilevel car Parking Construction Project by Microsoft India (R & D) Pvt. Limited, Sy. No. 210/1 and 203/P, Manikonda Jagir, Gachibowli, Rajendranagar (M), Rangareddy District, Telangana State Project/Activity-8 (b), Category 'B1' (2022), 1–284.
Faustina, J. (2022), How Telangana Subverted India's Land Acquisition Laws, *The Scroll*, November 22. Available at: https://scroll.in/article/1037993/how-telangana-subverted-indias-land-acquisition-law
Fish, C. (2011) Land acquisition for special economic zones in India, MA Thesis, temple University. Available at: https://scholarshare.temple.edu/bitstream/handle/20.500.12613/1220/Fish_temple_0225M_10580.pdf?sequence=1
Fuelling Growth: State Initiatives in the Data Centre Space (2022), *tele.Net*, May. Available at: https://tele.net.in/fuelling-growth-state-initiatives-in-the-data-centre-space/
Government Data on Cloud Must Be Stored in India: Ministry of Electronics and IT (2017), The Economic Times, April 21. Available at: https://economictimes.indiatimes.com/tech/internet/government-data-on-cloud-must-be-stored-in-india-ministry-of-electronics-and-it/articleshow/58288014.cms
Government of Telangana accelerates eGovernance through AWS (2022), *SME Street*, September 11. Available at: https://smestreet.in/technology/government-of-telangana-accelerates-egovernance-through-aws/
Graham, S. and Marvin, S. (2001), *Splintering Urbanism: Networked Infrastructures, Technological Mobilities and the Urban Condition*, Routledge, London & NY.
Graham, S. and Marvin, S. (2022), Splintering Urbanism at 20 and the "Infrastructural Turn" (169–175), *Journal of Urban Technology*, 29(1).
Hogan. M. & Vonderau A. (2019), The nature of data centres (1–3), *Culture Machine*, 18.
Hu, T-H. (2016) A prehistory of the cloud, MIT Press, Cambridge/London.

Hyderabad Data Centres, Data Centre Map. Available at: https://www.datacentermap.com/india/hyderabad/

Jena, G. (2022), The hidden environmental costs of India's data centre push, The Wire, May 14. Available at: https://science.thewire.in/environment/hidden-environmental-costs-india-data-centre-push/

Jha, M. K. & Jha, R. (2022) Data Centres in Nava Mumbai (128–165) from Manish K. Jha and Ritam Sengupta Eds. *Data Centres as Infrastructure: Frontiers of Digital Governance in Contemporary India*, Orient Blackswan Pvt Ltd, Hyderabad.

Johnson, D. A. (2010), Land acquisition, landlessness and the building of New Delhi (91–116), *Radical History Review*, 108 (Fall).

Kodali, S. (2023), 'BharOS vs Android: India Needs Not Just a Self-Reliant But Reliable Operating System, *The Wire*, January 23. Available at: https://thewire.in/tech/india-bharos-mobile-operating-system

Kumar, D. (2020), Why the smart cities mission needs an overhaul, The Citizen, November 27. Available at: https://www.thecitizen.in/index.php/en/NewsDetail/index/9/19670/Why-the-Smart-Cities-Mission-Needs-an-Overhaul---

Lele, S. (2022), Amazon Web Services Joins Telangana Govt with Cloud Adoption Framework, *Business Standard*, September 9. Available at: https://www.business-standard.com/article/companies/amazon-web-services-joins-telangana-govt-with-cloud-adoption-framework-122090901196_1.html

Levien, M. (2012), The land question: special economic zones and the political economy of dispossession in India (933–969), *The Journal of Peasant Studies*, 39 (3–4).

Mims, C. (2022), Google, Amazon, Meta and Microsoft Weave a Fibre-Optic Web of Power, *Wall Street Journal*, January 15. Available at: https://www.wsj.com/articles/google-amazon-meta-and-microsoft-weave-a-fiber-optic-web-of-power-11642222824

Misra, K. (2019), Accumulation by Dispossession and Electoral Democracies: An Analysis of Land Acquisition for Special Economic Zones in India (1–48), University of Mass: Amherst Economics Department Working Paper Series 274. Available at: https://scholarworks.umass.edu/cgi/viewcontent.cgi?article=1276&context=econ_workingpaper

MIST, Submarine Cable Networks, (n.d.) Available at: https://www.submarinenetworks.com/en/systems/intra-asia/mist

Mohanty, D., Khurana, A., Jain, M. & Arora, M. (2022) Data Privacy & Transfer in Investigations: India, Global Investigations Review, September 15. Available at: https://globalinvestigationsreview.com/insight/know-how/data-privacy-and-transfer-in-investigations/report/india

Moises, A. (2023) Digital Edge to Acquire 47-Acre Thane Land for Maiden Data Centre in India, *W.Media*, January 3. Available at: https://w.media/digital-edge-to-acquire-47-acre-thane-land-for-maiden-data-center-in-india/

Nandy, M. (2022), Blackstone Launces Data Centre Platform in Asia, Starting from India, *Mint*, November 16. Available at: https://www.livemint.com/companies/news/blackstone-launches-data-centre-platform-in-asia-starting-from-india-11668498459228.html

Narayan, D. (2022), Platform Capitalism and Cloud Infrastructures: Theorising a Hyper-Scalable Computing Regime (911–929), *EPA: Economy & Space*, 54 (5).

Nishant (2022), Why Amazon Wants the Indian Government by Its Side to Win the Cloud War, Outlook, January 11. Available at: https://www.outlookindia.com/website/story/business-news-why-amazon-wants-the-indian-government-by-its-side-to-win-the-cloud-war/409046

Pandey, M. (2022) Tracking Major Data Centres Announced in 2022, AnalyticsIndiaMag, December 8. Available at: https://analyticsindiamag.com/major-data-centres-announced-in-india-in-2022/

Peters, J. D. (2015) *The Marvellous Clouds: Towards a Philosophy of Elemental Media*, University of Chicago Press, Chicago.

Raj, Y. V. P. (2021), Hyderabad to Add Data Centre Capacity, *Telangana Today*, April 21. Available at: https://telanganatoday.com/hyderabad-to-add-data-centre-capacity

Rajeshwari, A. (2018), Microsoft Completes its First Solar Power Deal in India. Mercom. March 8. Available at: https://mercomindia.com/microsoft-solar-deal-bengaluru/

Regulatory framework for promoting data economy through establishment of date centres, content delivery networks, and interconnect exchanges in India (2021:1–186), Telecom Regulatory Authority of India (TRAI) Consultation Paper, 10/2021. Available at: https://www.trai.gov.in/sites/default/files/CP_16122021_0.pdf

Response to Consultation paper on regulatory framework for promoting data economy through establishment of data centres, content delivery networks, and interconnect exchanges in India (2022), TRAI – by STT Global Data Centres Pvt Ltd, February. Available at: https://www.trai.gov.in/sites/default/files/STT_Global_14022022.pdf

Ribes, D. and Finholt, T. A. (2009), The Long Now of Technology Infrastructure: Articulating Tensions in Development (375–398), *Journal of the Association of Information Systems*, 10(5).

Rohit, T. K. (2022), Panel Moots Separate Corridor for Submarine Cable System in Chennai, *The Hindu*, July 25. Available at: https://www.thehindu.com/news/national/tamil-nadu/panel-moots-separate-corridor-for-submarine-cable-system-in-chennai/article65682327.ece

Sathyanarayana, J. (2019), Enabling Data Science at Scale at Swiggy: The DSP Story, *SwiggyBytes TechLog*, November 9. Available at: https://bytes.swiggy.com/enabling-data-science-at-scale-at-swiggy-the-dsp-story-208c2d85faf9

Sattiraju, N. (2020), The secret cost of Google's data centres: Billions of gallons of water to cool servers, Time, April 2. Available at: https://time.com/5814276/google-data-centers-water/

Savills (n.d.). Available at: https://www.savills.in/services/land-services-for-data-centres.aspx

Sharwood, S. (2022), Google Integrates Indian Government's Cloud Services into Android, *The Register*, December 20. Available at: https://www.theregister.com/2022/12/20/android_india_digilocker_integration/

Shuja, J., Gani. A., Shanshirband, S., Ahmad, R. W. & Bilal, K. (2016), Sustainable cloud data centres: A survey of enabling techniques and technologies (195–214), *Renewable and Sustainable Energy Reviews*, 62, September.

Singal, N. (2023), India's Data Centre Industry: Here's Why the Sector Is Seeing a Flurry of New Players Joining In, *Business Today*, April 16. Available at: https://www.businesstoday.in/magazine/technology/story/indias-data-centre-industry-heres-why-the-sector-is-seeing-a-flurry-of-new-players-joining-in-376118-2023-04-05

Singh, A. (2022), States asked to fast track land allotment under industrial corridor plan, The Deccan Herald, April 22. Available at: https://www.deccanherald.com/national/states-asked-to-fast-track-land-allotment-under-industrial-corridor-plan-1103059.html

Supr Daily improves partner and customer experiences using machine learning on AWS (2022), SuprDaily by Swiggy, AWS. Available at: https://aws.amazon.com/solutions/case-studies/suprdaily-case-study/

Tamilnadu Data Centre Policy 2021. Available at: https://cms.tn.gov.in/sites/default/files/documents/TN_Data_Centre_Policy_2021.pdf

Velkova, J. (2019), Data centres as impermanent infrastructures (1–11), *Culture Machine*, 18.

Velkova, J. (2021), Thermopolitics of data: Cloud infrastructures and energy futures (663–683), *Cultural Studies*, 35 (4–5).
What's next for data centres: India (1–8) (2021), Cushman & Wakefield. Available at: https://cw-gbl-gws-prod.azureedge.net/-/media/cw/apac/india/insights/india-data-center-report_7_8_2021.pdf?rev=5650ff7f9818410a82688da6ed32bbb4

See also

Amazon Data Centre, 1600 acre Chandanavelly Industrial Park. https://www.youtube.com/watch?v=iEGFE9i2fNU

7 AI, Risk and The Gig Economy

The chapters in this volume taken together offer a critique of the GE in India. While there is a case to be made that both organised and unorganised work are good for the economy, the quality of work, just remunerations, work conditions, work security and compensation are all matters of concern, especially for workers in the unorganised sector that gig workers belong to. A real and relatively novel challenge for the GoI and other governments is that gig workers, unlike workers employed in the unorganised sector as agricultural labourers, in small firms or as casual labourers are managed primarily by algorithms and AI in the actualisation of their work and the compensations that they receive. This process of algorithmic management is in place precisely because of the regulatory arbitrage that platforms have been involved in and that has led to the establishment of their own rules of employment in a context in which there has been little or no regulatory history, rules and prior knowledge. It is only over the last few years that some governments, for instance, Spain (See Informacion Algoritmica:2022) and Germany (Doellgast et al.:2022) and regional bodies such as the European Commission (Eurofound), have begun to counter, and create rules for algorithmic management of work and workers, although these rules remain contested and variably implemented. In countries such as India where there is an over-supply of labour, gig work is celebrated as an Indian success story in reports made by NITI Aayog and think tanks and in the media.

The progress of AI in the Indian context is seen as natural since Indian populations have in the post-independent provided a captive population and employed knowingly or unknowingly in 'sandboxing' and experiments leading to the generation of large data sets helpful to research and development across multiple sectors including the medical sciences (See Samal and Chaterjee:2022). The National Digital Health Mission's (NDHM) Sandbox (2020) offers sandboxing in the following areas:

> '6.1.1. Products/Services • Utilization of Health ID, DigiDoctor Registry, Health Facility Registry, Personal Health Records, Telemedicine and Teleconsultation, e-Pharmacy, Health Clouds, and the Convergence and expansion of NDHM for Retail healthcare, Health Insurance and

DOI: 10.4324/9781003491705-8

> Health Assurance services, Healthcare Marketplace and aggregation, Digital KYC for healthcare, Healthcare/Health tech advisory services, Health management services, Digital health related identification services, Smart contracts, Healthcare inclusion products, Cyber security products, Products like Clinical Decision Support System (CDS), Research- Medical & Policy, Anonymization-as-a-service, Consent Management as-a-service
>
> (2020:15)

Sandboxing is of course an entirely legitimate process that is aimed at assessing the viability of say a fintech app without the benefits of regulation but under the supervision of regulators. It can enable an understanding of a potentially disruptive technology within a controlled environment based on tests that involve customers and trial and error testing – understandings that can be critical to both a company and provide regulatory knowledge before the technology is marketed and adopted.

However, there is some evidence from the field, that in the context of health care, a sector that traditionally has had a reputation for lax procedures related to clinical trials, that AI is being used in contexts where privacy and the need for consent are consistently ignored. Illancheran (2017) has highlighted the intervention of the Supreme Court in the halting of 162 trails from global pharma companies following the deaths of 2,644 volunteers in clinical trials between 2006 and 2013 in a context where there are no laws in place to monitor clinical research and drug trails (Antani & Gokhale:n.d. See also Motha et al.:2016). One of the stronger critiques of AI in the health industry in India is Radhika Radhakrishnan's (2021), a feminist critique of this industry. Based on the fieldwork in Karnataka and Tamilnadu and interviews with AI data scientists, healthcare personnel in four hospitals and clinics, patients and others, she explored the development of AI-enabled diagnostic systems. She makes three observations related to India being used as 'a testing pool for experimental AI technologies' (15). a) India's population diversity and disease diversity is attractive for locating 'algorithmic validation processes', b) 'data collection for training AI-enabled diagnostic algorithms is being combined with patient treatment' (16), thus reducing costs to the companies involved and c) these processes are being operationalised in the context of low patient understanding of their rights. Consent is often given because patients who are poor have little choice but to consent that in turn is construed as consent (17). Another issue that requires consideration is the growing number of AI alliances between Big Tech and diagnostic labs and hospitals in India such as that between Microsoft and SRL Diagnostics that is specifically in place because of the fact that Indian companies in the health industry do not have big data capabilities. Ultimately though, these alliances can be seen as a reflection of a battle between Microsoft, Google and Amazon for cloud business (Singh:2020). Made in India just does not make any sense in a context in which Big Tech has captured large parts of the data generated by Indian citizens.

The GoI and Risk

The GoI has explicitly committed itself to AI ethics and to the:

- the principle of safety and reliability;
- the principle of equality;
- the principle of inclusivity and non-discrimination;
- the principle of privacy and security;
- the principle of transparency;
- the principle of accountability; and

the principle of protection and reinforcement of positive human values, that mirrors the key requirements in the EU's White Paper on AI (2020:9. See also Responsible AI (2021:4) and Malhotra and Puhan:2023).

However, in light of the GoI's decision to not regulate AI (See No Plan to Regulate AI:2023) for the moment, that is in line with its belief that AI is a 'kinetic enabler', critical to the strengthening of India's AI capabilities and AI economy and to it becoming a market leader, it remains to be seen how the GoI will live up to its explicit commitments to AI Ethics. Despite this pronouncement, the GoI has indicated that rules related to AI will be included in the proposed Digital India Act (Proposed Digital India Act:2023) that will replace the Information Technology Act, 2000 (Sanzgiri:2023). Notwithstanding the fact that there are no privacy laws in place, the GoI has asserted that the requirement in the DPDPB, 2022 (that is yet to be passed in Parliament) that AI developers collecting larger amounts of data may be held responsible as 'data fiduciaries' for the ethical treatment of this data is a strong enough deterrent to a regulatory vacuum related to AI (See Bordoli:2023). However, given the fact that this bill is yet to see the light of day and in the context of what has been a very slow response by the GoI to the more egregious examples of algorithmic management adopted by delivery platforms such as Swiggy and ride-share platforms such as Uber and Ola such as fluctuating payments for work and hire and fire policies, the question as to whether they will respond positively to the needs of workers in AI-enabled environment remains an open one.

It would seem that the GoI has not invested a great deal in the anticipation of risks associated with AI.

Ulrich Beck, AI, and Risk

Risk is a real issue in the context of AI given the role played by machine intelligence in the shaping and operationalisation of production, logistics, distribution and production of goods and services across multiple sectors. When considering issues related to risk, it is useful to highlight concepts related to theory as proposed by German social scientist Ulrich Beck (1992) which was outlined in his classic study *The Risk Society*. Beck's work is particularly useful to this study because he also anticipates and deals with the changing nature of labour in the context of a post-industrial society, an issue that he deals with comprehensively in his 2000 study *The Brave New World of Work*. This book deals with trends that we now associate with the gig economy including the casualisation of work in the global economy and the development of contract work that is not accompanied by any of the work securities that are in place for workers in the formal economy. While Beck's work on risk was written just before the Chernobyl nuclear fall-out, it did correctly highlight the lack of preparedness in the anticipation of human-made catastrophes in an increasingly inter-linked, globalised world. There is an ever-present uncertainty and contingency about global risk whether it is global financial meltdowns or the real threat posed by global warming and climate change on the sustainability of life on earth. Beck points out that typically the State that is committed to reflexive modernity and the ideal of progress is reluctant or unwilling to take seriously the risks associated with new technologies.

> Once decisions on technological developments under the cloak of investment decisions have been taken, they acquire and develop, of course, a considerable weight of their own. Now they come into the world with the constraint that investments have about them – they must make money. Fundamental objections would endanger capital (and, of course, jobs). Anyone who now points out the side effects harms the enterprises that have invested their future and that of their employees in these plans, and thus ultimately endangers even the economic policy of the government. Therein lies a double limitation. Firstly, estimation of side effects occurs under the pressure of investment decisions taken in order to make a profit. Secondly, this is relieved by the fact that consequences are difficult to assess in any case, and governmental counter measures require a long path and a long time for implementation.
>
> (213)

So, the uncertainty, contingency and complexity of risk is often an excuse for governments to not respond to the invisibility of risk. Beck has also argued that in light of the universalisation of risk in contemporary society, individuals are left to deal with risks illustrated best by the small print consisting of waivers, disavowals and disclaimers that accompany our uses of services and products, from paints to mobile phones.

Beck (2006, 333–335) has argued in a subsequent article in the journal *Economy & Society* that global risk is characterised by de-localisation (its causes and consequences are omnipresent, it has a spatial dimension and has complex temporal and social effects over the long-term), incalculableness (one cannot predict its intensity or extensity) and non-compensatibility (meaning, that with the exception of planes being downed by a terrorist missile, we are faced with living life in a context in which it is close to impossible to remain safe against global risks. This has become the normal state of life. And all we can do is to take precaution through prevention. Non-compensation remains a reality in national contexts – and disasters such as the Bhopal gas tragedy exemplify risk that has been blamed on the negligence of the MNC, Union Carbide). In other words, in the context of a risk society and with the inability of authority such as the state or private sector to protect citizens from risk, it has increasingly become an issue for individuals to sort out themselves. The more we live in neoliberal economic environments, where innovations outpace regulation and the production of goods and services based on AI, machine intelligence and algorithmic management pose extensive risk to populations, the greater the onus on individuals to manage this risk. Drones using facial recognition software to identify demonstrators against unjust farming laws and other anti-citizen policies in India as well as the role played by algorithmic management in shaping work environments and work opportunities are examples of a technology that has, thus far, been able to function within what can be considered a 'lite' regulatory environment. The risk from unregulated AI is not just the quality of life and livelihoods of gig workers, but it needs to be seen in terms of both national and global risks that are outcomes of data – all transactional data being stored in data and cloud centres. When hyper-scale cloud centres such as Amazon's AWS increasingly becomes the space where both government–citizen and platform–citizen data are stored, risk is amplified precisely because these global data giants, despite obligations related to data localisation and their role as data fiduciaries, are difficult to police. Transparency and accountability of Big Tech are often at a surface level and do not go deep enough precisely because these companies are simultaneously global and at the same time so very entwined with the visions and functions of the Indian state. Labour market flexibility is key to this vision of neoliberal development that is celebrated in the NITI Aayog document on gig workers in the GE. Beck (2000:3), in a chapter on the Brazilianization of the West in his book *The Brave New World of Work*, highlights the risks associated with such labour markets in which just in time work replaces any long-term and secure labour.

> The upshot is that the more work relations are 'deregulated' and 'flexibilized', the faster work society changes into a risk society incalculable both in terms of individual lives and at the level of the state and politics, and the more important it becomes to grasp the political economy of risk in its contradictory consequences for economics, politics and society.

The EU, AI and Risk

While there are many valid reasons for the GoI's commitment to exploring AI efficiencies related to national mission–level projects, one of the questions that requires consideration is whether or not a laissez fair approach to AI-based innovations along with an explicitly anti-regulatory approach to AI is a responsible approach. In contrast to this, there is an explicit recognition of risk and levels of risk related to prohibited AI that has been the basis of the European Commission's proposed policy on AI (See Laying Down Harmonised Rules, 2021:5.2.2, page 12). The commission has proposed three levels of prohibited AI based on risk – 1) AI practices that are prohibited, 2) High-risk AI that needs close regulation and 3) low-risk regulation that needs to be flagged. The Policy includes 85 Articles and include the need for the need for data governance and management (Article 10), transparency (Article 13), accuracy, robustness and cybersecurity (Article 15) and trust that is a key cross-article consideration. This paper attempts to balance the interests of the State and the private sector with the rights of citizens – rights that are, in the last case, paramount. So, biometry-based identification in public spaces by enforcement authorities and the uses of FRTs are strictly controlled and only approved to be used to identify people of interest who pose a threat to national security rather than the general population.

> The use of AI systems for 'real-time' remote biometric identification of natural persons in publicly accessible spaces for the purpose of law enforcement is considered particularly intrusive in the rights and freedoms of the concerned persons, to the extent that it may affect the private life of a large part of the population, evoke a feeling of constant surveillance and indirectly dissuade the exercise of the freedom of assembly and other fundamental rights. In addition, the immediacy of the impact and the limited opportunities for further checks or corrections in relation to the use of such systems operating in 'real-time' carry heightened risks for the rights and freedoms of the persons that are concerned by law enforcement activities.
>
> (21)

While there are those who have argued that risk-aversion is not conducive to innovations in AI, risk is writ large when biometrics do not work and when FRTs wrongly implicate someone for a crime that she/he did not commit. These are not facile, merely academic issues but real issues that have real consequences for people. When algorithms based on machine learning are based on limited, exclusive or faulty data, it can have consequences for people who are different from the average mean. This is true for farmers whose biometrics can change – as is the case with thumb/fingerprints that can vary and lead to a non-recognition of Aadhar-based identification. There is, in other words, personal risk when machine learning is not able to capture the unique identifiers related to people. The EC's White Paper on AI (2020:11) explicitly highlights the consequences of AI for people who are vulnerable or marginalised:

> The use of AI can affect the values on which the EU is founded and lead to breaches of fundamental rights, including the rights to freedom of expression, freedom of assembly, human dignity, non-discrimination

> based on sex, racial or ethnic origin, religion or belief, disability, age or sexual orientation, as applicable in certain domains, protection of personal data and private life, or the right to an effective judicial remedy and a fair trial, as well as consumer protection. These risks might result from flaws in the overall design of AI systems (including as regards human oversight) or from the use of data without correcting possible bias (e.g. the system is trained using only or mainly data from men leading to suboptimal results in relation to women).

If this is a key issue, a second one is the security of data – and recent data breaches have exposed the risk of personal data spilling into the open to be used and abused. It is at the level of personal rights that the GoI's approach to AI falls very short. The lack of regulatory laws related to privacy and data protection may be economically and politically expedient, although it can result in the inability of the average citizen to be able to get legal support in the case of a data breach, biometric misidentification, denial of services and algorithmic discrimination that can affect all digital natives in India but specifically those whose livelihoods, are for the most part, controlled by algorithmic fiat. Gig workers, of course, are most vulnerable to the lack of legislations. While there is an argument that the availability of legislations, the mere existence of the many progressive legislations that are there in India are no guarantees for good practice, the fact that there is a legal framework in place that can be leant upon in times of stress, for example, when gig workers go on strike for better pay and working conditions, remains an important right for Indian citizens who are increasingly living lives in the embrace of a platform government and a platform economy. Existing legislations can be used by public interest advocates and NGOs to make the case for workers' rights. While the Constitution of India provides all citizens rights, over the last decade, those rights have increasingly come under threat from the current government's reinterpretations of these constitutional rights and their attempts to shape it in their own image. So, for example, the Citizen Amendment Act and the National Register of Citizens, 2019, were both attempts by the GoI to establish a majoritarian centred and mediated understanding of citizenship that favoured some minorities over the dominant minority group, Muslims. The Constitution also protects citizens against the wrongful uses of AI –for example, Article 15 prohibits discrimination on the grounds of religion, race, caste, sex or place of birth. There have also been major rulings supportive of the right to privacy, for example, in Justice K S Puttaswamy vs the Union of India where a nine-judge bench of the Supreme Court unanimously upheld the right to privacy as a fundamental human right that was critical to the rights of life, liberty, freedom and dignity (Koola:2022:1954), a right that is enshrined in Article 19 of the Constitution. The GoI's less-than-forthright response to its deliberate planting of the Israel-manufactured surveillance software Pegasus in the phones of 50,000 citizens that they considered 'anti-national' is just one of the examples of its attempts to curb civil liberties including the right to speech. This software inserts malicious codes into a smartphone's operating system, thereby controlling the device and taking over its content for the purposes of surveillance (Dhillon & Safi:2021).

As it has been highlighted in the chapters in this volume, the GoI's commitment to self-reliance and self-sufficiency (*Atmanirbhar*) seems to be a rhetorical ploy used for reasons of a populist kind. The reality suggests control over data by global Big Tech. Parminder Jeet Singh (2023), from *IT for Change* in a piece on the need to indigenise AI, uses the example of the Reserve Bank of India's call to develop AI-based supervisory technology to highlight the ambivalences and gaps in India's AI aspirations and practice

> .....the problem is that RBI has shortlisted seven foreign companies, one of which would eventually develop and likely run its AI operations. Relevant documents suggest that RBI may not have properly split the function into different components with a view to keeping overall control in-house. This might leave too much control in the hands of a foreign company. The system will be fed very sensitive financial data, on an ongoing basis. Such data in foreign hands is highly problematic. Most legal and contractual terms only limit the taking away of personal data. But the anonymised data provides patterns. Such exposure of India's sensitive financial data and intelligence is a serious issue

Similarly, while TikTok and other Chinese apps were banned in 2020, China's presence is real, be it in border states such as in Arunachal Pradesh, Chinese mobile phones sold in India and in the training of Foxconn workers in Tamilnadu. Viola Zhou and Nilesh Christopher (2023) in a fascinating article on Chinese engineers from Hon Hai Precision Industry (Foxconn), who have been flown to Chennai to help train an Indian workforce in the efficient production of iPhones, in particular, the iPhone15, have observed the factory at Sunguvarchatram is yet to become cost-effective in its production because of 'higher material costs and greater percentage of defective phones' – in other words, Chinese engineers involved in helping get 'the plant up to China speed'.

The Case for the Involvement of Civil Society in AI Policy-Making in India

AI offers so many possibilities to improve goods, services and increase productive efficiencies across many sectors including education, health, e-government, employment, agriculture and manufacturing, among many other services and productive sites. It also can be used to manipulate, discriminate, marginalise and control across a range of data-based services. It is this double-edged facility that gives AI a quality that requires regulation. So, as India embraces this brave new world, it is important that efforts are made to create a framework that enables AI potentials but that also disables and discounts an ethics-free approach to AI innovation. While the present government is not keen on inputs from civil society in the policy-making space, there simply is a need to create spaces for multi-stakeholder policy-making both at the level of the centre and that of the states. The fact remains that civil society in India has the experience, knowledge and skills on matters related to AI and there is an expertise in organisations such as the Centre for Internet & Society, IT for Change (Bengaluru), the Centre for Communication Governance at the National Law School, New Delhi, Digital Futures Lab (Goa) and advocacy thinktanks such as the Delhi-based MediaNama among other organisations. The strategic litigation done by the Internet Freedom Foundation (https://internetfreedom.in/legal/) at the level of the Supreme Court on issues including internet shutdowns, surveillance, website blocking, FRT, etc. is another example of civil competencies in the area of digital rights. The work was carried out by Rethink Aadhar, an organisation involved in exposing the limits to biometry-based identification linked to the Aadhar project. Their report of the death of a child to malnutrition in a village in Odisha in a family whose ration cards had been cancelled because of the mismatch of the name of the head of the household and his name on the Aadhar card (Fact Finding Report:2023) highlights the fallibility of biometry-based ID systems.

There are also a number of human rights organisations such as the People's Union Democratic Rights (PUDR) that have taken up the case for gig worker's rights (See PUDR Report:2021). Along with a number of gig worker unions whose work has been highlighted in the chapter on worker resistance, what these organisations have in common is a desire for digital justice, the rights of gig workers and the regulation of an AI-based economy in which citizens have rights to data privacy and the nation to data sovereignty. For the moment though, policy on India's digital future and its implementation is being carried out through public–private partnerships in which technocrats such as Nandan Nilekani, Arghya Sengupta and J Satyanarayana and a few favoured think tanks such as the Indian Software Product Industry Roundtable (iSpirit), the Vidhi Centre for Legal Policy and Khosla Labs are involved in national-level mission projects that have not been awarded on the basis of merit or that have undergone parliamentary scrutiny. Nileena (2020), in an article on these public–private partnerships, highlights some of the key players involved in creating the National Health Stack.

> Each health ID issued under the programme will be linked to a health-data consent manager, which is a set of APIs developed by iSpirit and the Swasth Alliance. The Swasth Alliance is a collaboration of 92 partners across health-tech companies, hospitals, diagnostic labs, insurance companies, tech companies, and venture capital firms including Apollo, Medanta, Onemg. The members of the alliance's advisory council include Amitabh Kant, the CEO of NITI Aayog; Indu Bhushan, the CEO of Ayushman Bharat and the National Health Authority; and Nilekani.

What Nileena has highlighted in this and other writings in *The Caravan* is the role played by a small group of private entities and individuals, who have a stake in the many projects associated with Digital India, who is involved in creating key digital architectures. They write the code that in turn becomes law rather than the law becoming the basis for code.

> Aadhar, and now Aarogya Setu demonstrates that instead of framing a law and then bringing in software and systems that run in accordance, India has followed the practice of engaging private entities to build software and applications, and then framing the laws to fit these systems.
> (Nileena:2020, 3. See also Thaker:2018)

While there is no doubt in the knowledge and skills of these people and organisations, their grand vision of platforming India and the GoI is primarily a technological solution where technology and business comes first and people's interests, be it privacy or the need for data to be security, is a secondary concern. More worryingly, the links between the government and these technocrats have increasingly become opaque and resulted in the emergence of a class of people described by Kavita Dattani (2020: 416) as 'governtrepreneurs' whose major interest is to invest in biometric services for welfare and financial services. As Dattani has pointed out, despite the case made by the GoI for the role of biometrics in the delivery of good governance and curbing financial leakages, the broader aim of the Stack is

> to develop a new customer-base for credit. Contributing to a 'governtrepreneurism', Aadhar and the India Stack, as new digital technologies of governmentality, reduce interactions between state and populations into digital transactions, enabling the weaving of corporate into government. In doing so, populations are transformed into subjects or customers of the corporate-state.
> (412)

As the GoI creates the data-citizen who is validated only if his ID is biometrically stable, how this utopia/dystopia will impact the workers in the informal and gig economies who are only nominally included in the database of India remains to be seen (Cohen:2019).

The GoI functions as a technocracy and is committed to a scientific-technological rationality. It believes implicitly in the power of experts and hence all the investments in public–private partnerships in the making of Digital India. The fact that they discount legal-procedural rationality is clearly highlighted in the manner in which it has gone about creating and executing national-level connectivity projects without due process such as getting parliamentary approval or getting a range of stakeholders involved in the making of such projects. There is a sense in which technocrats are in a hurry to initiate projects, unencumbered by bureaucracy or the need for dialogue and discussion, that they feel are unnecessary time-wasting stumbling blocks to projects that they believe result in national efficiencies such as in the disbursement of welfare entitlements. This has led to a coterie of experts wielding power over decision-making and who are shielded from any public scrutiny or from requirements of transparency and accountability. Esmark (2017:503) has observed that technocrats are typically anti-politic and anti-ideologic. Although, in the case of India, this technocracy has bought into the techno-nationalist project of connectivity and the platformisation of the GoI. On the one hand, the technocratic project is strongly opposed to the established ideologies of parliamentary and democratic politics. On the other hand, scientific management can be said to constitute an ideology in its own right insofar as interest in politics is supplanted by a 'politics of expertise' where political decisions are presented as necessary interventions above political contestation and debate.

On 5 July 2023, the parliament approved the DPDPA after a six-year lag (ETtech:2023). The fact that the DPDPA affirms the right of the state to be the final arbiter of data in India highlights the shortfalls that exist in the technological policy in India. A 2023 report on the Digital Infrastructure for Knowledge App (Diksha), an educational app owned by the central government has revealed that children's data has been transmitted to a third-party company without the consent of parents or children and that a data breach has led to millions of IDs of teachers and students being made available in the public domain (Thanawala (2023). It is important that such policy, be it the proposed Digital India Act, the National Deep Tech Start-up Policy and emerging policy on AI or in other areas, is created for the *right reasons*, is *secure*, is based on *transparency and accountability* and that its benefits and guarantees *make a difference* in the lives of the working classes in India, including platform-linked gig workers. While the Rajasthan Platform-Based Gig Workers (Registration and Welfare) Bill's, 2023 ambit includes all data aggregators (digital intermediaries) and is a step in the right direction, aggregators are not defined as employers; there is a lack of clarity related to the rights to gig worker mobility and the disbursement of social security payments to workers by state and central governments remains opaque (Banik:2023). The lack of a range of social securities for gig workers despite the enactment of the Social Security Code in 2020 remains a major concern although arguably this lag cannot be considered unusual in a country where the implementations of laws are typically constrained by witting and unwitting delays. The Social Security Code, while a step in the right direction, does fall short since it distinguishes the rights of employers and their mandatory benefits such as gratuity, provident fund, etc. from those of gig workers whose social security benefits have been left to the design whims of individual state governments and the central government. There is hope that gig worker securities will be included in the Union Budget 2024, although there can be no guarantees in the context of other more pressing political priorities in an election year. In such circumstances, worker resistance is absolutely critical as it can lead to aggregators being forced to concede to worker demands. Ideally though, a combination of gig worker rights defined by their work with their 'aggregator employers' along with clear access to state and central insurance and other subsidies will enable optimum worker security outcomes for gig workers in India.

Bibliography

Algorithmic Management, EurWork, Eurofound. Available at: https://www.eurofound.europa.eu/observatories/eurwork/industrial-relations-dictionary/algorithmic-management

Antani, M. & Gokhale, G. (n.d.), Issues and concerns in conducting clinical trails in India, Pharma Focus Asia. Available at: https://www.pharmafocusasia.com/clinical-trials/issues-concerns-conducting-clinical-trials

Banik, N. (2023), Necrocapitalism and the dark side of India's gig work economy, East Asia Forum, September 23. Available at: https://eastasiaforum.org/2023/09/23/necrocapitalism-and-the-dark-side-of-indias-gig-work-economy

Beck, U. (1992) *Risk Society: Towards a New Modernity*, Sage, London.

Beck, U. (2000), *The Brave New World of Work*, Polity, Cambridge and Malden.

Beck, U. (2006) Living in the world risk society, *Economy & Society*, 35 (3), 329–345.

Behind the veil of algorithms: Invisible workers: A report on workers in the 'gig' economy (2021:1–15), PUDR, December. Available at: https://pudr.org/sites/default/files/2022-01/PUDR%20report%20on%20gig%20workers-%20Behind%20the%20Veil%20of%20Algorithms.pdf

Bordoloi, P. (2023), India backs off on AI regulation. But why?, TechCrunch, April 10. Available at: https://analyticsindiamag.com/india-backs-off-on-ai-regulation-but-why/

Cabinet approves Digital Personal Data Bill (2023), The Economic Times, July. Availableat:https://economictimes.indiatimes.com/tech/technology/cabinet-approves-draft-data-protection-bill/articleshow/101517561.cms

Cohen, L. (2019), India as database: response to Reetika Khera (328–340), *Contributions to Indian Sociology*, 53 (2).

Dattani, K. (2020), "Governtrepreneurism" for good governance: The case of Aadhar and the India Stack (411–419), *Area*, 52.

Dhillon, A. & Safi, M. (2021), Indian Supreme Court orders enquiry into state's use of Pegasus software, The Guardian, October 21. Available at: https://www.theguardian.com/news/2021/oct/27/indian-supreme-court-orders-inquiry-into-states-use-of-pegasus-spyware

Doellgast, V., Wagner, I., O'Brady, S. (2022), Negotiating limits on algorithmic management in digitalised services: cases from Germany and Norway, *European Review of Labour and Research*, 29 (1), 105–120.

Esmark, A. (2017), Maybe it is time to rediscover technocracy? An old framework for a new analysis of administrative reforms in the governance era (501–516) *Journal of Public Administration Research and Theory*, 27 (3).

Fact Finding report on alleged malnutrition death of a child in Ghatisahi village of Jaipur district (2023:1–8). Available at: https://drive.google.com/file/d/1ovJtLc5ozu6IedOmn_M0LsYpy4m-P-gB/view

Illancheran, M. (2017), Measuring the impact of reforms on India's clinical trial environment, Clinical Leader, October 12. Available at: https://www.clinicalleader.com/doc/measuring-the-impact-of-reforms-on-india-s-clinical-trial-environment-0001

Informacion Algoritmica en al ambito loboral (2022:1030), Goberno de Espana, May. Available at: file:///Users/uqpthom4/Downloads/algortca_laboral.pdf

Internet Freedom Foundation. Available at: https://internetfreedom.in/legal/
Koola, S. J. (2022), Legal regulation on artificial intelligence in India: A human rights perspective (1992–2001), *International Journal of Law Management & Humanities*, 5 (2) Pp 1991–2001.
Malhotra, A. & Puhan, B. (2023), India: Artificial Intelligence Comparative Guide, TMT Law Practice, Mondaq, June 13. Available at: https://www.mondaq.com/india/technology/1059762/artificial-intelligence-comparative-guide
Motha, C.S., Nalini, R., Alamelu, R & Amudha, R. (2016), The moral calculus of pharma companies in India, *Asian Journal of Pharmaceutical and Clinical Research*, 9 (2), 30–33. Available at: file:///Users/uqpthom4/Downloads/admin,+Journal+manager,+14_AJPCR_10445_REV.pdf
NDHM Sandbox: Enabling Framework (2020), National Digital Health Mission, August 18. Available at: https://abdm.gov.in:8081/uploads/sandbox_guidelines_b39bcce23e.pdf
Nileema, M. S. (2020), Is India privatising governance through partnerships in public digital infrastructure, The Caravan, October 20. Available at: https://caravanmagazine-in-nalsar.knimbus.com/policy/is-india-privatising-governance-through-partnerships-public-digital-infrastructure
Nileena, M. S. (2020), From Aadhar to Aarogya Setu, Vidhi's questionable role in technology-related policy making, The Caravan, August 26, 1–18.
No Plan to regulate AI, IT ministry tells Parliament, The Hindu, April 5. Available at: https://www.thehindu.com/news/national/no-plan-to-regulate-ai-it-ministry-tells-parliament/article66702044.ece
Proposal for a Regulation of the European Parliament and of the Council: Laying down harmonised rules on artificial intelligence (Artificial Intelligence Act) and amending certain union legislative acts (2021:1–108), European Commission, Brussels, April 21. Available at: file:///Users/uqpthom4/Downloads/regulation_ai_875509BF-C386-0D30-2CB7E56A798BA4EA_75788.pdf
Proposed Digital India Act (2023), Digital India Dialogues, Bengaluru. March 9. Available at: https://www.meity.gov.in/writereaddata/files/DIA_Presentation%2009.03.2023%20Final.pdf
Radhakrishnan, R. (2021), Experiments with social good: Feminist critiques of artificial intelligence in healthcare in India, *Catalyst*, 7 (2), 1–28.
Responsible AI: #AI for All. (2021), Approach document for India, Part 2: Operationalizing Principles for Responsible AI, Niti Aayog, August. Available at: https://www.niti.gov.in/sites/default/files/2021-08/Part2-Responsible-AI-12082021.pdf
Rethink Aadhar. Available at: https://rethinkaadhaar.in/testimonials
Samal, M. & Chaterjee, P. (2022), Regulatory Sandboxes for Artificial Intelligence: Techno-Legal approaches for India, ISAIL-TR-002 (1–37), Indian Society for Artificial Intelligence and Law, April 14. Available at: https://issuu.com/indiansocietyai/docs/isail-tr-002_online
Sanzgiri, V. (2023), MeitY minister Rajeev Chandrasekhar talks about AI regulation under the Digital India Act, Medianama, May 25. Available at: https://www.medianama.com/2023/05/223-meity-chandrasekhar-ai-regulation-under-the-dia/
Singh, P. J. (2023), An 'Atmanirbhar' AI will benefit India. Here's why, IT for Change, April. Available at: https://itforchange.net/an-%E2%80%98atmanirbhar%E2%80%99-ai-will-benefit-india-here%E2%80%99s-why
Singh, S. (2020), Google, Microsoft circle as India mulls extracting value from health data of 1.3 billion citizens, *The Ken*, January 6. Available at: https://the-ken.com/story/google-microsoft-india-pdp-health-data-sharing/
Thaker, A. (2018), The new oil: Aadhar's mixing of public risk and private profit (1–39), The Caravan, May 1.

Thanawala, S. (2023), Serious allegations emerge against Diksha app for breach of personal data of millions of teachers and school students, The Leaflet, Feb. 17. Available at: https://theleaflet.in/serious-allegations-emerge-against-diksha-app-for-breach-of-personal-data-of-millions-of-teachers-and-school-students/

Vidhi Centre for Legal Policy, Gig Workers. Available at: https://vidhilegalpolicy.in/blog/tag/gig-workers/

While Paper on Artificial Intelligence – A European approach to excellence and trust (2020:1–27), European Commission, Brussels, February 19. Available at: https://commission.europa.eu/system/files/2020-02/commission-white-paper-artificial-intelligence-feb2020_en.pdf

Zhou, V. & Christopher, N. (2023), Indie Foxconn's struggle to make iPhones in India, November 28. Available at: https://restofworld.org/2023/foxconn-india-iphone-factory/

Index